# A GOOD LEADER SO HARD TO FIND

ARVIND UPADHYAY

Anyone who has studied leadership knows there is no shortage of information available on what it supposedly means to be a good leader. Discussions on leadership are everywhere. A quick scan of the internet will produce an untold amount of material—some scholarly, some from the business world, and some from a variety of companies designed to help organizations improve their leadership capacity. Professional development courses and degree programs are also available to help people become eff ective leaders. Despite all the resources available on leadership, it seems we are still experiencing a leadership vacuum. Th e concepts of good leadership, it appears, are not getting through. Over many years the authors have asked a variety of people informally to identify fi ve exceptional leaders they have come across: individuals who truly exemplify eff ective and admirable leadership. Most people cannot complete the task. Some struggle to identify a single individual they know, whom they respect as a truly excellent leader. Almost without exception, those individuals considered as possibly good leaders are identifi ed as having one signifi cant defi cit or another. At the same time, the people we questioned did not struggle to come up with examples of truly bad leaders. And they were not very forgiving in their assessments. Th is phenomenon of the bad leader and the horrible boss is so prevalent that it inspired a Stanford professor to write about them. Dr. Robert Sutton's Th e No Asshole Rule became a New York Times bestseller, and created such a response that he wrote Good Boss, Bad Boss to continue the discussion. It is hard to fathom how bad leaders and bosses can survive in a world fi lled with volumes of leadership advice, but they do. Th at there are so many poor leaders tells us we still have much to learn on the leadership front. Th e truly horrible leaders and bosses that Sutton describes are only one contribution to the leadership vacuum: there are others.Our intent, however, is not to continue the critique of bad leaders. Our agenda is a more positive one, and this is to continue the search for good leaders, and what it takes to become one. Specifi cally, this book is our attempt to identify the things a person should attend to if they want to be a truly eff ective leader. In detail, it may seem like a long list, but the items we identify and discuss fall under six domains we refer to as the BASICS, an acronym we will explain later in this chapter. Th ere are other approaches to the leadership issue, with one guru aft er another usually referring to some magic number of traits that a person needs to be a good leader. Th ose lists, however, are usually made with reference to leaders in the private sector. Our framework, and this book, is directed to people who work in the public sector. We would argue that leadership for these individuals is oft en more complicated and thus requires a comprehensive discussion, which we consider to fall under the BASICS. We would also argue that there is a very practical reason to think in terms of the detailed structure we provide here. Sometimes you can only know whether someone has a particular characteristic by the presence of an associated collection of other related characteristics. Before getting into the BASICS, though, it is important to ensure we agree about what constitutes good leadership. Accordingly, we will fi rst discuss what we mean by leadership, the purpose of leadership, what is so special about leaders in government, and why the BASICS are important. Furthermore, we will discuss why we keep coming back to our central idea of the inner core of a good leader. What is Leadership? When we look at the various defi nitions and ideas about leadership, it is not hard to conclude that the concepts of leadership are all over the map. For example, some adherents uphold concepts of servant leadership. Others talk about visionary leaders. Other terms, such as transformational leadership, also show up in the literature. And there are lots more. Th ere are also defi nitions that draw a distinction between leadership and management, with some displaying a sense that being a leader is somehow superior to being a manager. In reality, most leaders engage in some form of management, and all managers should demonstrate leadership. Even employees who are not in management display leadership among their colleagues and teams.

For us, one way to see the diff erence is this: We lead people, but we manage tasks. Management relates to the processes that keep an organization functioning, such as planning, budgeting, defi ning roles, and resourcing and measuring performance.1 Leadership is about aligning people with the vision, inspiring them, motivating them, and providing eff ective communication. Leadership is about relationships.2 Leadership is also about infl uence. As one leadership guide3 notes: When your management hat is on, you are focusing on how you are going to complete the tasks that are necessary to get the job done. You see the deadline looming, and you organize yourself to meet it. When your leader hat is on, you are infl uencing the others on your team to do their part to meet—or exceed—that deadline or any other performance expectations you might have. Our concept of good leadership includes both leadership and management as expressed above.

Management is doing things right; leadership is doing the right things.Peter F. Drucker

Th en there are those who work from the perspective that leadership is accessible to everyone, as the natural expression of a fully functional personality.5 It has also been noted that some forms of work require one to shift into leadership mode when the need arises, even though the person is not normally considered a leader. An example here might be fl ight attendants on an airplane: most of their time is spent serving their passengers, but in an emergency, they immediately switch into a directive, leadership role to ensure every passenger's safety. In the public sector, police offi cers and fi re fi ghters also have this dual role. In one sense they exist "to serve and protect," but they also provide strong leadership in crisis situations. So much so, that many people believe that every offi cer is a leader.

# Contents

# Foreword

While we appreciate what we can learn from these diff erent understandings of leadership, this book is not intended to advance one leadership theory over another. What is important, in our view, is for people who have responsibility for getting a job done (or part of a job done) to have certain skills, abilities, and aspirations that help them get that job done well. Not only that, good leaders must also be able to facilitate the eff ort and commitment of their colleagues, employees, and stakeholders to achieve the task. We recognize that even those who have lead roles in getting a job done are oft en commonly reporting to someone else or working with an outside party. Our premise is that all workers in an organization, despite diff erences in position or title, are fellow workers and colleagues. We also acknowledge the important role of internal and external stakeholders for government. Getting any job done involves individuals or groups who may not be involved in accomplishing the task or providing the service, but may have an interest in the process or outcome. Th at interest needs to be respected. The Purpose of Leadership Obviously, leadership needs to be more than simply working with others to get a Job done. If that werc the only purpose, we would have to say that many people who have senior roles in the Mafi a, drug cartels, and terrorist organizations are good leaders. Certainly, many of them have good track records of getting the job done. But in getting the job done, they disrespect people, they deceive people, they hurt people, they break the law, and they generally work in a dictatorial manner. Likewise, history has shown us time and time again that someone can rise to become the leader of a country, be successful at staying the leader for some time, and be referred to as a leader, but that does not mean they have any signifi cant admirable leadership characteristics. Th ey can lead by positioning themselves as powerful bullies. In short, they can be successful in getting a job done without having genuine leadership skills. As we note, the purpose of leadership involves more than getting a job done. It involves getting it done in a certain way—a way that shows a genuine respect and concern for the well-being of everyone who has a stake in completing the job or task at hand. To do that, one needs consistently to behave in a certain way. Further, prospective leaders need to have a certain set of aspirations and skills behind those behaviours, and they need to hold strong information, communication, and sustainability commitments.

## The purpose of leadership involves more than just getting a job done. It involves getting it done in a certain way.

Good Leaders With the above in mind, being a nominal leader, even a so-called successful one, is not necessarily anything to be proud of. Being a "good' leader, however, is a much diff erent thing. A good leader is someone who embraces and consistently demonstrates a broad range of leadership attributes as a foundation for the way in which they work to get a job done. Th ey understand that it is not just about meeting a mandate or achieving a stated goal, but that it is equally about the process of working with people and their interests to get there. Importantly, they understand that the process of working with people requires credibility, consistency, and sustainable buy-in. Most importantly, a good leader understands the characteristics and attributes needed to be a good leader, works to develop those attributes in themselves and those who report to them, and appreciates how consistency helps to defi ne the working culture of an organization. What then are the attributes of a good leader? In this book, we have tapped into extensive research from a wide variety of sources in business, academia, government, and the larger public sector. Many of these sources have a particular focus or a favoured set of attributes that they claim makes a good leader. However, we want to look specifi cally at what is needed for those working in various levels of government. Th erefore, we have adapted what is coming from elsewhere to be relevant to this unique context.

B ehaviours

A spirations

S kills

I nformation Commitments

C ommunication Commitments

S ustainability Commitments

of Good Leadership.

As we noted at the beginning of this chapter, we have developed a list of attributes that we consider to be the BASICS of good leadership, and each of those is linked to a letter of our acronym. Each chapter will explore these in turn. However, you will also learn that the six letters—Behaviours, Aspirations, Skills, and Information, Communication and Sustainability commitments—are all generated from and supported by the inner core of the good leader. Th is inner core is the part of a person's character that relates to ethics, integrity and values. To help anchor this concept, the diagram below displays this with the inner core as the centre of the wheel. You will notice that in each successive chapter, the centre of the wheel remains constant. Th at is because, for every area, the inner core of a good leader has a role to play.

As we think about these concepts, it is important to note that we are not encouraging people to become perfect leaders. We realize that as people we are all fallible, and no one can get it right all the time. We all have limitations. While it may not be possible for us to attain perfection, it is quite reasonable to aspire to be a good leader. Th at is realistic and it is doable. It is within the reach of every person to learn how to be a good leader. But here is the key. Good leadership is only possible if it fl ows from a strong inner core of good character and ethical thinking. More than ever, organizations are crying out for leaders who are responsible, principled, ethical, and have the courage to do the right thing. Our world is fraught with environmental challenges, issues of social responsibility and justice, and deep needs that aff ect how all of us live—now and into the future. We need government leaders who not only have the skills and behaviours of good leadership, but who guide their work with a moral compass and an ethical, principled core. Th e BASICS of good leadership in government is based on this premise. In Chapters One and Two, you will see how the behaviours of good leaders are anchored in and expressed through this strong inner core. Th ese behaviours of good leaders are expressed in various domains relating to how we work with others, how we create and express vision, how innovative and courageous we are, and how we achieve results. In Chapter Th ree we see how aspirations diff er from behaviours. Th ese are within the heart and mind of a leader, and link with the longer-range goals and hopes we have for our own growth as a leader. Aspirations help us move from where we are to where we want to be. Aspirations link with our values, beliefs, principles, and ethics. In Chapter Four we explore the skills that are needed to do the job in everyday settings. In Chapters Five, Six, and Seven, we look at the commitments that good leaders make. A commitment is more than an aspiration; it is a decision and promise you make within yourself to behave in a certain way, in a consistent and dedicated manner. Th is is about consistency, and living out certain principles and values in a way that aff ects the outcomes as well as the organizational culture. Th ese commitments show up in three key areas: information, communication and sustainability. In these chapters we will look at the ways that a strong inner core will aff ect our leadership. Before we get there, though, let us start with a deeper exploration of the inner core of a good leader. As we have said, the behaviours, aspirations, skills, commitments of good leaders fl ow from this inner core, and it is impossible to become a good leader without it.

# CHAPTER ONE

# The Inner Core of a Good Leader

**Leadership is a potent combination of strategy and character. But if you must be without one, be without the strategy.Norman Schwarzkopf**

The inner core consists of the intrapersonal (i.e., self-concept, character, values, references, beliefs, thoughts, emotions) and interpersonal elements (i.e., behavioral tendencies) that strongly impact how effectively you acquire and cultivate the nine outer-core leadership competencies. Usually, people see, experience, and pass judgment on your outer core. The inner core, though critical in driving the outer core, is hidden. People don't observe your self-image, beliefs and references. They observe only your behavior. Predictive relationships exist between your inner and outer core. If you possess a strong inner core, you have a heightened capability to acquire, grow, and mature in the development and evidence of the competencies and skills comprising the outer core.

Another unique tool in the book is the Map of Leadership Maturity. You identify nine different types of leaders:

The Perfectionist

The Helper

The Entertainer

The Artist

The Thinker

The Disciple

The Activist

The Driver

The Arbitrator

I haven't met anyone who doesn't enjoy figuring out his or her primary style, then analyzing the boss. Would you take us through "The Map" to give us a flavor of how it works?

Of course! The Map of Leadership Maturity grew from my earlier research and consulting work in the middle 1990s and my first book, Success Yourself, which I believe was the first book written applying the concepts of the Enneagram to the world of business. In the past 15 years, I have refined my ideas and concepts based on my continuing research as well as my experiences coaching over 250 leaders in that time. "The Map" is a powerful tool that provides leaders with the framework and roadmap for exploring and distinguishing between the nine distinct predominant traits defining great leadership. It helps leaders gain a granular understanding of the degree of maturity that they must possess in the values, thoughts, emotions, and behaviors of their own predominant trait as well as in the other eight traits that comprise their unique leadership fingerprint. They learn that being a successful leader is less a function of their predominant trait and much more a function of the relative maturity with which they evidence that predominant trait—and each of their other eight traits. They learn specific strategies on how they can strengthen their maturity within all their traits. They also learn specific strategies for building rapport, trust, and credibility with individuals who present a different predominant trait from theirs. In addition to learning key insights about their leadership styles, they build knowledge and skills so that they can more successfully lead different style types. Ultimately, in writing this book, my sincere desire is that leaders and future leaders begin to recognize, appreciate, and internalize that unlocking and unleashing their own leadership potential is a function of possessing a passionate and diligent desire to:

Discover their unique development goals and strategic developmental pathways.

Begin executing these strategies with passion and focus.

Learn and course-correct continuously as they execute with passion and focus.

What are you seeing as you work with leaders from all industries with these new tools? Anything surprising? Do most people know where they fit?

Yes, most people are pretty accurate in identifying their predominant trait, however, they are not nearly as accurate in identifying their maturity levels. For example, if a particular leader discovers that their predominant trait is "Perfectionist", they get excited because the assessment in the book, "The Mattone Leadership Enneagram Inventory (MLEI)," has confirmed what they already knew about themselves. But, the key to leadership growth and growth in general is uncovering four areas:

(1) indisputable strengths

(2) indisputable development needs

(3) surprise strengths; and

(4) surprise development needs.

The MLEI assessment (inner core assessment) combined with a multi-rater or 360 leadership assessment (outer core assessment) provides the pathway for all leaders and future leaders to clearly identify these four areas. In my experience, the absolute key to a leader unlocking their potential is in identifying the "surprises"...both positive and negative. So, back to the Perfectionist example: While they are excited that the MLEI has accurately identified their predominant trait, they may become surprised that the MLEI has also identified that they possess more immature elements of perfectionism (i.e., dogmatic, inflexible, enjoy proving others wrong, unattainable goals, can "rationalize" their actions to maintain their "logical" position, can be cruel and sadistic) as opposed to the more mature elements (i.e., self-disciplined, realistic goals, can tolerate others' shortcomings, can evaluate problems and determine priorities). This becomes an important breakthrough for leaders to discover. Most organizations in their leadership development efforts are falling short when it comes to having leaders and future leaders "look inside" at the health and vibrancy of their inner core. We need to do a better job at helping leaders and future leaders become "vulnerable"...in my experience working with executives it is vital that we help them come to grips with the fact that while they might be effective leaders and future leaders....they are not the absolute best they can be. When a leader accepts and internalizes this sometimes difficult truth, this becomes the first step to unlocking their greatness as a leader.

What is at the Core of a Good Leader? Whether we have given it much thought or not, each of us is guided by a world view, belief system, or code of values that infl uences our decisions, how we meet our needs, and how we interact with others. Researchers have observed that the most eff ective leaders are guided by a strong set of principles, ethics, and a moral framework that enables them to function with integrity, transparency, honesty, compassion and consistency.8 In fact, this inner core of ethics and integrity is an essential component of being seen as an authentic leader—one whose inner values visibly align with their behaviour in a way that inspires trust and confi dence and commands respect.9 Th ese leaders walk the talk. Th is is especially important in times of crisis, when maintaining the public trust is vital.10 However, trust and respect are most oft en earned in the hard grind of daily operations when a leader shows consistency, good judgment, and principled character day to day.

The older I get, the more I understand that leadership is all about one word: Trust. If you have the trust of your colleagues and the people you are leading, then and only then, can you accomplish great things. But trust needs to be earned each and every day. In my experience, you build that trust in three simple ways: fi rst, listen carefully; second, do the little things right; and fi nally, do what you say you will do. Glen Clark

Th e boss or supervisor who is in the "horrible person" category probably does not have many of these attributes and behaviours. In contrast, researchers have also observed that an ethical leader will not only behave ethically, but they will infl uence, consciously and unconsciously, followers to behave honestly and ethically as well.13 Th is helps create an ethical work culture, in which these values and principles are embedded in how the work is done. Functioning daily in an ethical, professional way is not just about judgement and decision-making. It also includes a regard for others, including intentionally helping and respecting the rights of others, an awareness of social obligations such as respecting cultural norms and values, as well as performing duties appropriate for a given social position, and it involves recognizing personal responsibility.14 Th is seems like a pretty tall order. In a culture that is becoming more and more individualized, subjective, and less concerned about traditional or moral absolutes, it can be challenging for emerging leaders to determine what it means to be ethical and how to develop that aspect of who they are. However, given that the work of government has a direct eff ect on the lives of people, it is an essential exercise for those who work at any level of government.

Here is an example from the health care system. Dr. Eileen Morrison,15 a professor of health administration who teaches ethics to government health professionals, points out that administrators are the stewards of the resources that society has invested in health care, creating structure and support for the health care system. Stewardship involves the careful and responsible management of resources entrusted to one's care, and is an important component of ethical leadership. Morrison teaches that leaders in health care must not only excel in the tasks of administration, but they need a deeper understanding of the principles of ethics and appropriate behaviour from an individual, organizational, and societal perspective. She encourages leaders to develop their ethical framework to help them know individually what is right and what is wrong, and to develop it at the organizational level, to ensure there is an appropriate code of conduct and standard for acceptable behaviour for all. She also speaks of the importance of an ethical framework that goes beyond the organization to include higher-order, societal perspectives. What Morrison is saying applies to other government departments as well, and her work (along with others) can help us explore and defi ne our ethical framework. In the specifi c world of health care, what might this look like? Let us take an example of how ethics on an individual level can also translate to the organizational and societal level. In North America and other parts of the world, a component of a physician's ethical practice is to fi rst do no harm. Th at will guide the physician (and other medical practitioners) to ensure they only act in ways that are in the patient's best interest, and will not cause harm to the patient in their eff orts to help or treat. Th at will infl uence how they intervene—or do not intervene. However, on an organizational level in an increasingly over-burdened health care system, how do we implement the philosophy of fi rst do no harm with organizational and systemic problems such as long wait times or overcrowded emergency rooms? We know that long wait times and overcrowded emergency rooms can increase the potential harms for patients.

Ethics should be ingrained in each and every pore of organizational life. Mihelič, et al.

What about situations where people with greater fi nancial resources are better served than those without? What about the pressure to treat and manage conditions in ways that generate more revenue for pharmaceutical companies, or profi ts for practitioners? And as society's values shift and change, how do we preserve medical ethics that may run counter to the requests of special interest groups? Or, as needs grow but resources are limited, how do we respond to the confl ict between providing care and meeting the budget? Good leaders need to think through the implications for the individual, for the organization and for broader society, to ensure that their branch of government is providing service that meets ethical standards at both the individual and the collective level. Ethical dilemmas can be found in virtually every area of government service, in addition to health care. Leaders, with their greater degree of infl uence and responsibility, are generally held to higher standards of moral accountability. Anyone who intends to infl uence others to act in a specifi c way to achieve an identifi ed objective is morally accountable for the way in which the infl uence was exercised, and its foreseeable consequences.17 For police and fi re services, which have paramilitary hierarchies, it is understood that rank or position increases one's responsibility exponentially.18 Accountability and moral responsibility increase with a promotion to a higher level of authority and responsibility for others, a reality that good leaders take seriously. Accordingly, good leaders guide themselves with a fi rm commitment to respect others and preserve human dignity, with a commitment to justice and human rights. Th is can help prevent abuses and unfair treatment. Th ey also have a broader view that takes the needs of society into account. What does this look like? In some departments of government, it may mean they will not allow pollution to go unchecked. In others it could mean taking steps to prevent corruption from tainting the relationship between government and business, where there may be incentives to behave unethically in how contracts are awarded. It could also mean ensuring two-way communication with those directly aff ected by government action.

Organizational ethics also demonstrate themselves in how the people within the organization have collectively agreed to conduct themselves. More and more, organizations are enhancing their mission and vision statements with a set of core values that serve as a guide for how the work is done. Organizational values say, "Here's who we are and what values are important to us. Th is is how you can expect us to behave." However, it is up to each individual worker to exemplify those values, and to undergird them with their own inner strength of character and ethical thinking. Without an ethical and moral framework, this is diffi cult to accomplish. Ethical leadership also requires an understanding of the values and norms of society. Without this, some leaders in government have made serious errors that have harmed others, tarnished their own reputations, and have jeopardized the relationship of trust that exists between government and the public. In summary, the inner core of a good leader must be grounded in ethical thinking and a strong moral anchor.

Social Responsibility: Our Values Go Public More than ever, the public is looking to business and government leaders to demonstrate greater concern for others and less concern for their own self-interest. For most people, this is another dimension of ethical leadership. Businesses are also concerned about being good corporate citizens, and many have made great contributions to the communities that support them. Increasingly, successful businesses are focusing on what has been dubbed the triple bottom line, where concern is given to a company's economic value as well as its social responsibility and its environmental impact.19 But what does social responsibility mean when you work for government? And how does it connect with this idea of the inner core of the good leader? Even though the work of government is essentially all about working for the people, public cynicism and disenchantment with politicians and the government still abounds. Th is should encourage leaders in the public service to seriously consider how they can help change that perception. Social responsibility is enhanced when leaders combine eff ective listening and communication with concern and respect for the needs of others. Social responsibility contributes to the organization's reputation, culture and positive perception, both internally and externally. It conveys that the organization values fair practices within its sphere and at the locations where it operates.

Philanthropic community service is oft en the public face of a private corporation's social responsibility strategy. Th is speaks to the need to look beyond the walls of the organization to what sort of contribution the organization is making to the larger world. For government, though, they are already concerned about serving the public. Th is means that governmentfocused social responsibility goes beyond community service (their primary reason for existing) to include relationship integrity and ethical practices such as transparency in fi nancial reporting, ethical treatment of employees, clients and stakeholders, practising conservation, renewal and sustainability eff orts, and fi scal prudence to ensure tax revenue is used responsibly. Social responsibility means making the choice to do the right thing.21 Good leaders are socially responsible, function ethically and take good care of people and resources inside and outside their organization, as an extension of their personal integrity, their ethics, and their values. Th ey genuinely care about the negative impacts of practices and decisions on people. For leaders who work for government, this means they care about people who work for them and the people whose lives will be aff ected by decisions governments make. Th is requires a principled and compassionate approach, to ensure that the process of achieving goals and objectives does not create harm to those internal or external to the organization. Th is may involve how human resources are managed within government; it might also be about government programs that have a signifi cant impact on people's lives, the environment, or how funds are allocated. Th e inner core of the good leader will drive the leader's aspirations, ensuring that they achieve positive results in ways that are principled and attuned to the needs of others, not just for their own personal goals or agenda.

**Leaders with a strong sense of character and humility have a sense for doing the right thing because it is the right thing, not because they expect something in return. Ken Blanchard**

Th e eff ective leader is a transparent and consistent person, whose inner strength is based on ethics, integrity and honesty. Th ey walk their talk. Th ey make ethical decisions guided by a strong moral compass. Th ey are socially responsible. Th ey ensure their organization or department is guided by values and a code of conduct. Th ey understand and respect the societal values and norms that are relevant to their work. Th is forms a foundation for other leadership behaviours that refl ect the heart and mind of the leader. Building on that inner core of an ethical, moral framework, good leaders are motivated by a concern for others, and have a desire to serve in a way that empowers, supports, and inspires those who follow.23 As the name suggests, the civil servant is there to serve. Th is implies service to the public, to key stakeholders, to those in authority, and to those entrusted to the leader's care. Th is may seem counter-intuitive, when it seems the workers are there to serve the requirements of the leader. However, leadership theory demonstrates that good leaders also serve those who work for them, through a variety of key mechanisms. What does this look like? Th e following chapter examines several visible behaviours that are grounded by an inner core of good character. As we will see, these are essential strengths for the successful, good leader.

# CHAPTER TWO

# Behaviours of Good Leaders

*What is the test of good leadership? To do the right thing, at the right time, for the right reason, in the right way. It's not enough to know what to do; it also matters how and when you do it, and what motivates you.*

I n Chapter One we talked about the strong, inner core of ethical thinking and moral character that is at the centre of good leadership. In this chapter we are going to look at the principle that doing fl ows from being —the idea that our behaviours fl ow from and are generated by the values, principles, morals, and ethics that guide our actions and choices. Th ere are many behaviours that are associated with good leadership, and we have clustered them into six areas. From our perspective, good leaders are collaborative, they care about people, they are good listeners and communicators, and they are results-focused, visionary, innovative and courageous. Th is is illustrated in the diagram on the next page.

## Being collaborative is a key aspect of a good leader.

Unlike traditional models of authoritarian or 'command and control' leadership, the outer circle represents a new trend in leadership, in which vision and direction are set by a leader who also empowers, supports, and listens to those who follow that vision. It is a collaborative model of leadership that empowers and engages the workforce, inspiring them to follow. For this reason, being collaborative is near the top of the wheel.

Collaboration and community engagement are dynamic practices taking hold in all levels of government and throughout the not-for-profi t and charitable sectors. We also see that alternative dispute resolution mechanisms, collaborative resolution processes, inclusive approaches, and team-based structures are becoming more and more the norm in business, the social sector, and in certain areas of government. It only makes sense for the civil service to respond in kind, adopting and adapting practices that have yielded success in other sectors of our society. To become a collaborative leader, one must fi rst embrace the values that undergird a collaborative approach:

inclusion • empowerment • fairness • balance • creativity • a desire to work eff ectively and cooperatively with others to solve problems and accomplish goals

According to the Ohio Community Collaboration Model,24 collaboration requires new types of leadership styles and structures, in which power, authority and responsibility is distributed across the group. Healthy collaboration fosters shared commitments, helps resolve confl icts, facilitates lasting relationships and stimulates eff ective action. It requires new structures and team approaches rather than individual approaches. Team members collaborate and organizations (and departments) develop partnerships in support of this new way of doing business. It is characterized by give-and-take, trust, and shared responsibilities.

Not only that, collaborative processes encourage consensus-building, confl ict resolution mechanisms, shared information systems, and shared decision-making systems. Th is can be very challenging in a work environment that is hierarchical by nature, or where departments have functioned independently of each other and of the community at large.

However, the benefi ts of collaboration are well documented and worth considering:25 • improved communication among participating organizations • increased job and life satisfaction for professionals • increased resources and better utilization of them • improved service integration, coordination and delivery • improved access to and faster delivery of services • increased cost effi ciencies, through reducing duplication or fragmentation of programs An eff ective leader must be committed to building the relationships necessary to sustain the collaboration. Th is involves listening to the partners, encouraging open and ongoing communication, clarifying needs and interests, and developing a strategic action plan that will be evaluated and renewed in an ongoing way.26 Th is sounds like a lot of work, and it is. However, trust is a natural outcome when there is eff ective communication between partners, when people keep their promises, and when confl icts are addressed and reframed as they occur. 27 Collaborative processes are fi nding favour in all levels of government in a variety of places. As one example, the Government of Canada has identifi ed collaboration as a key component of engaging and mobilizing people, organizations, and partners.

I know of no single formula for success. But over the years I have observed that some attributes of leadership are universal and are often about fi nding ways of encouraging people to combine their efforts, their talents, their insights, their enthusiasm and their inspiration to work together. Queen Elizabeth II

## Leaders must be focused on results and relationships. Ngang

Behaviour #2: Demonstrate a Genuine Concern for the Well-being and Success of Colleagues and Associates Behaviour #3: Invest in People, Ensuring They are Supported and Developed Research demonstrates that eff ective leaders are not just collaborative, but they have a cluster of "people skills" that enable them to lead with compassion, empathy, and concern for others.31 Th is supportive approach is grounded in showing respect for the ideas, experiences and contributions of others, and with the humility needed to invite input, both positive and constructively critical.32 Th ese soft skills are a kcy component of building trust with followers, who need to feel respected, included, empowered, and heard.33 Realistically, it is not always possible to be collaborative—it depends on the needs of the situation. While the eff ective leader knows when to collaborate and when to make an executive decision, those executive decisions will be easier for followers to accept if the day-to-day culture is respectful, supportive, and where appropriate recognition is given to the ideas and contributions of other people.

Th ere are benefi ts in behaving this way. Leader support is associated with higher levels of employee satisfaction, well-being, and lower levels of intention to leave.35 In a study of more than 1,400 leaders, managers, and executives, eff ective communication and people management were identifi ed as the top two skills needed, followed by empathy and emotional intelligence as the third most important skill set for leaders.36 Th ese soft skills really matter. Th e leader's ability to put others before themselves, to empathize, to seek to understand, to build rapport, and to show concern, allows them to build positive connections with their direct reports and others.37 In contrast, it is helpful to note the top fi ve things that leaders most oft en fail to do when working with others. Interestingly, most of these also relate to the use of soft skills.38 1. Failing to provide appropriate feedback (praise, redirection) 82% 2. Failing to listen or to involve others in the process 81% 3. Failing to use a leadership style that is appropriate to the person, task, or situation (over-supervising or under-supervising) 76% 4. Failing to set clear goals or objectives 76% 5. Failing to train and develop their people 59% Th e business world depends on leaders with soft skills because these leaders attract and retain top performers, and they motivate employees to contribute to the organization. Th ey know that improving quality and motivation of human capital increases the company's competitive advantage.39 Government also needs to attract and retain top talent to handle the complexities of government administration. Generous salaries, benefi ts and pension plans are one way to improve retention, but those elements on their own do not create a workplace culture that enables workers to thrive and perform with excellence. Good leaders do that. Employees need leaders who invest in them, encourage their growth and development, and give them opportunities to shine.40

Research indicates that the number one reason leaders succeed is the quality of their relationships... In other words, people do not leave organizations, they tend to leave leaders.41 Chalmers

Behaviour #4: Demonstrate a Commitment to Getting Results Repeatedly, the research literature stresses the importance of being results-focused.42 Aft er surveying 189,000 people in 81 diverse organizations, the McKinsey's Organizational Health Index identifi ed four key behaviours associated with leadership eff ectiveness:43 • solving problems eff ectively • operating with a strong results-orientation • seeking diff erent perspectives • supporting others Th e researchers noted that "leadership is not only about developing and communicating a vision and setting objectives, but also about following through to achieve results. Leaders with a strong results orientation tend to emphasize the importance of effi ciency and productivity and to prioritize the most important work."44 A results-oriented approach in business is ultimately about the bottom line: is the company producing a profi t? Governments have a diff erent focus, and defi ne their success in diff erent terms.

Results-based management has been adopted by Western democratic governments to provide greater accountability and transparency regarding taxpayer contributions.45 Designed to measure performance by results, it improves performance through making changes to how the organization operates so results will improve. Stakeholders are included and involved in defi ning realistic, expected results, in assessing risk, in monitoring progress, in reporting on performance and in integrating lessons learned into management decisions.46 For many government organizations, this is oft en about designing and implementing programs that achieve certain goals or create certain benefi ts for the public. Clearly, being results-focused needs to be anchored and balanced by the other key components of ethical decision-making, concern about people, and eff ective communication to ensure that results are achieved without collateral damage. Th e end does not justify the means! Good leaders strive for excellent results without compromising their values and other people in the process. Th e soft skills of leading people and the task-oriented skills associated with results-focused leadership are complemented by the fi nal component that includes vision, innovation, and courage.

## If decision-making is a science, judgment is an art.47 Zimmerman & Kanter

Behaviour #5: Have Vision Behaviour #6: Encourage Innovation Not everyone is fortunate to have a charismatic, dynamic personality, but eff ective leaders do have a sense of vision. Th ey see possibilities and strategic opportunities, and use those in innovative ways. Th ey create a compelling vision of the desired future for the organization and communicate it in a way that others can follow.48 Specifi cally, this involves translating their vision and goals into the language of each person, and then integrating it into their everyday job.49 Ideally, the mission and vision then become the worker's personal goals.50 Th eir daily eff orts become a means of bringing the mission and vision to life. However, the more layers of administration or bureaucracy there are between the visionaries at the head of an organization and the front-line employees who deliver the actual services, the more diffi cult it is to see the mission and vision translated to the employees.51 Th is requires that leaders at every level of the organization have the capacity to articulate the vision and successfully infl uence the performance of their team while making the mission and vision relatable to their team members on a personal level.52 In summary, a successful leader has a clear sense of vision that can be translated into goals and an action plan, and who has the listening and people skills needed to provide eff ective guidance, support and recognition.

Kouzes & Posner53 determined fi ve complementary behaviours that were eff ective at defi ning good leadership practice: 1. Model the way. Lead by example, and make certain that people adhere to agreedupon standards. Follow through on commitments and build consensus around the organization's values. Ask for feedback on how your actions aff ect people's performance. 2. Inspire a shared vision. Describe a compelling image of the future, noting trends that infl uence the work. Appeal to others to share the dream; paint the "big picture" of group aspirations. Speak with conviction about the meaning of the work. 3. Challenge processes. Search outside the organization for innovative ways to improve, and challenge people to try new approaches. Ask, "What can we learn?" Make certain that goals, plans and milestones are set; experiment and take risks. 4. Enable others to act. Develop cooperative relationships; actively listen to diverse points of view. Treat people with dignity and respect; support decisions other people make. Give people choice about how to do their work and ensure that people grow in their jobs. 5. Encourage the heart. Praise people for a job well done and express confi dence in people's abilities. Creatively reward people for their contributions and recognize people for their commitment to shared values. Find ways to celebrate accomplishments and give team members appreciation and support. Th ese fi ve behaviours demonstrate how a commitment to vision integrates well with the leader's character, task-focused skills, and interpersonal skills. Th ey also show the importance of courage and innovation in the leader's thinking.

**Power isn't power at all—power is strength, and giving that strength to others. A leader isn't someone who forces others to make him stronger; a leader is someone willing to give his strength to others that they may have the strength to stand on their own.54 Beth Revis**

Behaviour #7: Lead with Courage Vision needs to be supported by innovation and courage to bring it to fruition. Frequently, having vision means challenging the status quo. Nevertheless, having the courage to revisit "sacred cows" and suggest better paths toward the future can be diffi cult. Taking action on performance issues also requires courage. Th e eff ective leader confronts reality head on. Only by knowing the true state of your organization can you lead it to a better place.55 Courageous leaders face the facts, seek feedback and listen, and say what needs to be said.56 Th ey also encourage push-back: constructive dissent and healthy debate oft en reveal that in the tension of diverse opinions lies a better answer.57 When it is needed, they take action on performance issues and prevent toxicity by reassigning or exiting underperforming employees, for the sake of the team and the organization.58 Eff ective and courageous leaders lead change, and they communicate openly and frequently. Th ey make decisions, move forward, and give credit to others along the way. And fi nally, they hold themselves and others accountable, and model the behaviours they expect.59 At some point, every organization or government will face a crisis of some magnitude. Th ese are prime examples of complex situations that tax the capabilities of even the most eff ective, courageous leaders, so it is worth talking about them. Unfortunately, it is oft en the handling of a crisis that leads to more damage than the crisis event itself.60 Crisis leadership is more than managing corporate communication and public relations; while these are necessary, they are not enough to lead an organization through a crisis.61 Crisis leadership is about building a foundation of trust within the organization and with key stakeholders as well, and leveraging the crisis situation as a means for creating organizational change and innovation.62 Establishing trust is oft en done by taking full responsibility and making an apology, with a description of the actions taken to make things right. Truthful communication supported by value-laden actions helps the leader restore public confi dence, because open, honest leaders are more believable in a crisis.63 Once again, this speaks to the importance of a strong inner core of ethics, principles, and a strong moral compass.

Leading with courage in a crisis also requires the ability to see beyond the negatives to the opportunities in the situation. Good leaders apply lessons learned to ensure the organization will be revitalized and improved aft er the trauma of the crisis has subsided. Even though it is diffi cult to weather the storm, a crisis can bring issues to the attention of the leadership that have been overlooked or neglected. It presents opportunities for innovation and system improvements, which will benefi t the organization in the future. Adopting this positive approach helps courageous leaders move from feelings of anger, anxiety, guilt and despair to optimism and hope.64 A leader who adopts this approach will be able to apply these principles to less stressful situations as well. Summary As we consider the BASICS of leadership in government, we have seen that it involves internal qualities and commitments, and external behaviours and skills. Simply put, the leader is concerned about people and concerned about the work. Guided by vision, ethics and values, with a commitment to being socially and personally responsible, the leader guides and infl uences others toward achieving the goals of the organization. Th e leader is resultsoriented, making sound, well-informed decisions because they listen, gather information, ask questions, foster dialogue, and take input. Strategic analysis and eff ective task management are accompanied by a strong concern for the people on the team. Eff ective leaders invest in their people, ensuring they are supported, developed, respected, included and recognized. Working collaboratively with others, they harness creative energy and foster innovation, with enough toughness and courage to ask the hard questions and challenge the status quo.

## Good leadership involves both internal qualities and commitments, and external behaviours and skills.

Good leaders: 1. foster genuine collaboration 2. invest in people, ensuring they are supported and developed 3. have a genuine concern for the well-being and success of colleagues and subordinates 4. commit to getting results 5. encourage innovation 6. have vision 7. are courageous: they are able to make really tough decisions

# CHAPTER THREE

# The Aspirations of a Good Leader

**The aspirations of good leaders link closely with their values, and express themselves in their goals and in their choices.**

While Chapters One and Two are focused on the inner core and behaviours of the good leader, now we are going to think about what good leaders aspire to be. Th e aspirations of good leaders link closely with their values, and express themselves in their goals and in their choices. Aspirations relate to what we hope to achieve as a leader, what we personally aim or strive for. Th is is not about organizational development—these are personal aspirations we carry with us no matter what job we are doing. Our aspirations give us personal goals to keep striving for, to focus our professional growth and development. Our aspirations will infl uence our daily actions and behaviours, yet in another sense, they remain ahead of us, always a little out of reach. You'll notice that in our BASICS model for this chapter, the inner core remains the same. As always, the inner core of ethics and moral principles will guide the leader and shape their behaviour, their aspirations, how they use their skills, and how they respond to their information, communication, and sustainability commitments. Th e outer ring refers to the aspirations that we will be discussing. Starting near the top of the wheel, the good leader thinks in terms of "getting to yes." Th ey understand that successful negotiations involve exploring and striving to meet the needs of all aff ected parties to the best degree possible. Even though it might not always be possible, they still aspire for win-win solutions and outcomes because those work best to meet needs and preserve relationships. Building bridges between groups, fi nding solutions that work, and striving to build on common ground—these are so important in government that we have placed this circle near the top of the wheel. Th is builds on our earlier discussion of the importance of collaboration in the behaviours of good leaders. Following that are aspirations that are expressed daily in the attitudes, values, and behaviours of good leaders. Before we look at those, though, let's consider further how character and ethics relate to a leader's aspirations.

How Does a Good Leader Create an Ethical, Values-based Work Culture? It is not enough for a leader to be personally principled and ethical; good leaders establish a principled, ethical workplace with a code of conduct and a system of moral principles and values that are implemented across the organization. Th is enables them to lead with a moral compass. It is the ability to transform, direct, and guide culture that is the essential element to ensuring the organization continues to function within its ethical guidelines. Part of creating an ethical, values-based culture begins with the leader's own moral compass, defi ned as "a set of moral principles, informed by a sound conscience, reinforced by repeatedly acting in accord with those principles."65 Moral leaders are people who: "live by a deep moral code which has been slowly nurtured over a lifetime, and consistently demonstrate moral leadership by the way they navigate the challenges life throws at them. Such a code of moral behaviour is guided by a cultivated conscience which is aligned with timeless human values, rather than a set of social codes of 'moral' conduct as articulated by a particular faith group or culture."66 However, moral relativism has made it diffi cult to articulate and defi ne these timeless human values, being more concerned about the rights of the individual, and the subjective and individualized sense of what is right and what is not. Th is exposes governments, business, and society at large to signifi cant moral risk.67 Th is can be mitigated by the recruitment and cultivation of leaders with a strong inner code and moral compass, and processes that help establish the principles, values and moral code that will guide the workplace. Leaders with a strong moral compass will not only do the right thing, but they will also call others to moral action. Good leaders aspire to uphold high principles and values, and guide others around them to upholding those values as well.

**Great leaders move us. They ignite our passion and inspire the best in us. When we try to explain why they are so effective, we speak of strategy, vision, or powerful ideas.**

**But the reality is much more primal. Great leadership works through the emotions. Daniel Goleman, on "Primal Leadership"**

Aspirations #1 & 2: Demonstrating a Commitment to Getting to Yes, with a Commitment to Seeking Win-Win Solutions In Chapter Two we discussed the importance of a collaborative leadership style, pointing out the many benefi ts of working in collaboration with others to achieve organizational goals. In this chapter, we want to look deeper at this, in terms of the aspiration of the leader to "get to yes" with others in a way that is collaborative, interest-based, and focused on win-win outcomes. Where did this idea of "getting to yes" come from? In 1981, Roger Fisher and William Ury69 published an infl uential book that changed the way we understand confl ict and negotiation all around the world. Even those who have never heard of them or their book have heard the expression "getting to yes," without knowing the source. Much of the alternative dispute resolution fi eld has been built on their ideas, and mediators today frequently use the interest-based, collaborative approach Fisher and Ury fi rst wrote about so persuasively. Personnel from government and the private sector frequently take confl ictresolution workshops that contain ideas that originally came from Fisher and Ury's Getting to Yes. Signifi cant global confl icts have been reduced when negotiators have adopted this way of addressing the issues.

William Ury is a co-founder of Harvard's Negotiation Program and Distinguished Fellow of the Harvard Negotiation Project. He has served as a mediator and advisor in negotiations ranging from wildcat strikes to ethnic wars around the world. Like Fisher, Ury was also a consultant to the White House, and has published numerous books that continue to shape this dynamic and growing fi eld. Th ese two know what they are talking about. What are their key ideas and how are they especially useful for those in government? Now in its third edition, Fisher and Ury's book describes what they call the "negotiation revolution."70 A generation ago, the prevailing view about decision-making was hierarchical. Th ose at the top made the decisions; those lower down followed their orders. Today's world is characterized by fl atter organizations with less hierarchy, faster innovation, and the connectivity coming from the internet. We are now linked and connected to many other people over whom we have no control at all. To accomplish our work and to meet our needs, we cannot simply rely on giving orders. To get what we want, we are compelled to negotiate. Th ey have observed that the "pyramids of power are shift ing into networks of negotiation."71 For most people, negotiation evokes the idea of winners and losers. Aft er generations of heated labour disputes, positional bargaining sessions, legal battles, and strikes, that view is not surprising. To reach an agreement in this style of negotiating, someone has to give in. Fisher and Ury have helped re-defi ne what negotiation can look like by encouraging a cooperative approach that creates benefi ts for both sides. In their view, "there are cooperative ways of negotiating our diff erences and that even if a 'win-win' solution cannot be found, a wise agreement can oft en be reached that is still better for both sides than the alternative."72 Th is approach harmonizes well with what we have already discussed about the importance of collaboration. When people work together collaboratively—looking out for the interests of the other as well as their own interests and striving to fi nd mutually-agreeable solutions to the best degree possible —confl ict is reduced. Fisher and Ury's approach is not to eliminate confl ict; in contrast, they suggest that confl ict is an inevitable and useful part of life. It oft en leads to growth in insight, new perspectives, and positive change. Few injustices are addressed without confl ict. And confl ict is at the heart of the democratic process, where the best decisions are made by exploring diff ering points of view and searching for creative solutions.

We discussed earlier that good leaders encourage debate and healthy dissent, and this is why they do so. You need to hear all those diff ering perspectives to be able to really understand the needs, interests and values that are at stake. Th en you can explore, together with the aff ected parties, what a good outcome would look like and why. Th is issue is not whether confl ict arises; the leadership challenge is how to handle it when it does. For Fisher and Ury, "Th e challenge is not to eliminate confl ict but to transform it. It is to change the way we deal with our diff erences—from destructive, adversarial battling to hard-headed, side-by-side problem-solving. We should not underestimate the diffi culty of this task, yet no task is more urgent in the world today."73 As Fisher and Ury put it, the challenge for good leaders is to be "soft on the people" while remaining "hard on the problem." Th is is diffi cult: our human nature inclines us to stick with people who agree with us or support our views, and we do not tend to like people who disagree with us. It is annoying to be in a confl ict. Th at frustration can lead us to mistreat people, rather than deal with the real underlying issues. Understanding Positions and Interests Th e reality is that each day is full of decisions and moments when we can choose to act alone in a directive manner, or we can choose to cooperate and collaborate with others. While making the executive decision is appropriate in many situations, it is increasingly important for leaders to take input from a variety of sources, and use that information to guide their decision-making. When issues become contentious, it is extremely important for leaders to be able to discern what is NOT being said, as well as what is on the table. What do we mean by this? Generally, people put their positions out fi rst, e.g., "We need a raise" or "We have to cut the budget." Th e positions people hold are the judgments, opinions, or solutions that they feel best meet their unspoken, underlying needs and interests. Th ese positions can become very infl exible and entrenched, as is evident in many labour confl icts. Two parties trying to negotiate their positions usually do not fi nd a win-win.

When issues become contentious, it's extremely important for leaders to be able to discern what is NOT being said, as well as what is on the table.

Underneath the visible, spoken positions are the oft en unspoken needs, interests, values and beliefs that have shaped their positions. Th is is really the heart of the matter, and a wise leader knows to explore these thoroughly before negotiating a solution. People are very reluctant to make agreements that force them to compromise or jeopardize their needs, interests, values or beliefs. Th e best agreements represent creative solutions that meet these underlying needs for both parties to the greatest degree possible. Stephen Covey, the well-known author of Th e Seven Habits of Highly Eff ective People74, called this "and" logic, describing it as the foundation of win-win agreements. Instead of one side winning at the expense of the other, with "eitheror" outcomes, this is "a way of thinking and interacting that seeks constantly for mutually and maximally benefi cial, creative, third-alternative solutions."75 It balances the needs of one with the needs of the other, seeing through the lens of "and" rather than "either-or". The Iceberg Metaphor: Shifting from Positions to Interests Th e diagram on the next page creates a picture of what confl ict or disagreements oft en look like. As we know, icebergs sit deep in the water, with only a small portion of the ice showing above the waterline. It is very diffi cult to tell how big an iceberg is if you only look at it from above. However, as we know from the tragic story of the Titanic, it is what is below the waterline that sank the ship. In other words, our positions, solutions, opinions, emotions, and judgements are like the ice showing above the water. Th is is what catches one's attention. Below the water are all the needs, interests, values, beliefs, fears and hopes that have caused us to form our proposed solution to the problem. Th is is a much larger but unseen portion of the iceberg. What is under the water holds up what is above the waterline, but it is largely invisible to those looking at the iceberg from a distance. Eff ective communication involves uncovering those hidden interests. As people share these needs and values, it becomes possible to shift away from their demands or solutions to a deeper understanding of why the confl ict really matters, and what it is truly about. Once these interests, needs and values are revealed, it becomes easier to look for common ground, and shared needs and values. You can then also identify the diff erences that exist. Meaningful discussion is now possible to allow for a collaborative spirit of brainstorming to fi nd the options and solutions that are the best fi t for both parties.

Th e communication skills used in this kind of exploration involve open questions, use of empathy, identifying issues in a neutral way, and the use of skills such as paraphrasing, summarizing, clarifying, and reframing. Many leaders develop these specifi c skills through negotiation and communication training off ered as professional development. However, it is not enough just to develop the techniques of interest-based negotiation. Skills development must be balanced with a mindset that truly values this collaborative approach, with a genuine concern for the needs of others. Otherwise, the leader will appear insincere or half-hearted in the desire to fi nd those win-win solutions and outcomes.

Solutions OPINIONS Positions Judgments ASSUMPTIONS EMOTIONS interests Unmet needs BELIEFS VALUES Hidden / unspoken

Aspiration #3: To Inspire, Motivate and Affirm In Chapter Th ree, we talked about visionary, innovative, and courageous behaviours that are part of good leadership. Th e aspirations of a good leader include the desire to inspire others, to motivate them to excel, and to affi rm them for their eff orts. Th is is part of creating a winning culture76 in which people not only know what to do, but they know why they should do it. Companies and organizations with successful, high performing workplace cultures recognize that their values need to be embraced at every level, and that workplace culture is fi rst established and modelled by the leadership.77 Good leadership ensures that the vision and values are clearly articulated so they can be easily followed, building on the example set by the leader. In terms of productivity, a good leader inspires followers to excel over and over again. Th eir energies are focused on external customers and competitors, rather than on internal issues of politics or "turf." Transforming workplace culture takes time and focused energy, but a good leader knows in the end the most persuasive results of creating a "winning culture" will be seen on the frontline.78 Th is requires not just motivation, but also affi rmation and encouragement from the leader to ensure the successful behaviours of the team will be repeated. Good leaders communicate with the followers in mind: they speak in ways that connect with followers, they collaborate, they listen and they engage their followers to align with the organization's goals and vision.79 Th ey also support their employees, which is a signifi cant factor that increases employee well-being and productivity.80 Th e aspirations of the good leader will include the desire to inspire, motivate and affi rm others through a supportive, collaborative approach.81 Research indicates this is positively associated with higher levels of employee satisfaction, well-being and workplace productivity.

A good leader will aspire to create a "winning culture" in which people not only know what to do, but why they should do it.

Aspiration #4: To Strive for Excellence Good leaders inspire their followers, but to what end? One of the aspirations of the good leader is not only to strive for excellence on a personal level, but to inspire their followers to strive for excellence as well. In Chapter Two we talked about the results-focused leader, who sets objectives and achieves results. Th e aspirations of thc good leader defi ne those results in terms of achieving excellence, whether that relates to the quality of programming provided, the nature of service delivery, or how the particular branch of government fulfi lls its mandate. For government, this can also include streamlining processes and reducing red tape, reducing wait times, increasing effi ciency to benefi t the public, or ensuring an excellent experience at each touchpoint with taxpayers and society at large. Excellence is linked with the values associated with the work. One cannot do excellent work without knowing fi rst what matters, and having a sense of an external standard or guide. Good leaders want their organization or unit to be second to none. Th ey want the product or services they provide to be second to none as well. Th is requires setting a high standard, and inspiring staff through a positive approach to achieve it. Aspiration #5: To be Optimistic and Positive Having an optimistic outlook is one of the attributes of a likeable, emotionally intelligent leader. Research data shows that optimistic, positive, approachable leaders are seen in a more positive light by those who work for them than leaders who possess other innate attributes such as intelligence.82 What is the good news? Th e attributes of a likeable leader are under the leader's control, and can be cultivated by anyone. You are not necessarily born with them. According to Dr. Travis Bradberry from Talentsmart83—an organization that studies and specializes in emotional intelligence—the 10 key attributes of leader likeability include numerous points that relate to positivity and optimism. Talentsmart's research shows that a likeable leader is relational, approachable and humble, and maintains a positive outlook. Th ere is a positive energy and enthusiasm about them that is infectious. People enjoy being around other positive people. In contrast, negativity drags people down. Positive, likeable leaders appreciate the potential in those around them. Th ey see the best in others, and they help others to see the best in themselves. Th ey are encouraging. Th ey draw out people's talents so that everyone is bettering themselves and the work at hand. Th ey see opportunities where others see challenges; they remain hopeful even when the going is tough. Th ey also possess the interpersonal skills to develop good relationships and inspire employees.

Optimism is not only good for those around the leader, but an optimistic outlook has direct benefi ts for the leader, too. Not only do optimistic people tend to earn more than their pessimistic peers,85 optimistic people also enjoy an array of positive health outcomes, improved levels of subjective well-being, better health, and more success.86 Optimistic people have better coping mechanisms for handling and recovering from stress.87 In short, it is good for both your health and your career to be optimistic. Humour and laughter seem to fl ow right alongside those who have a positive, enthusiastic outlook on life. It is not always easy to see the lighter side of things but it certainly is helpful. Optimism serves as a social lubricant that lightens up the mood and generates positive, good feelings among others. Laughter has its own health benefi ts: it increases heart rate and blood fl ow, with similar benefi ts to exercise.88 Endorphins are released through laughing, which help to relieve pain, reduce cravings and stress, and slow the aging process.89 Laughter can help to reduce blood sugar levels, improve the immune system, and increase our antibodies that fi ght disease.90 Th e optimistic, positive leader knows that times of laughter and fun in the workplace contribute to creating positive energy and happy employees. Researchers have learned that emotions generally are infectious —just like the common cold. You can "catch" an emotion just by being in the same room with someone, through a subtle, non-verbal process. "Since emotional leads tend to fl ow from the most powerful person in a group to the others, when the leader is angry or depressed, negative body language can spread like a virus to the rest of the team, aff ecting attitudes and lowering energy. Conversely, happy and buoyant leaders are likely to make the entire team feel upbeat and energized.

Like negativity, positive energy is infectious. People watch their leaders, and body language says more than we realize. Eff ective leaders pay attention to their non-verbal signals, and use positive motivation to inspire their workers. In contrast, negativity signifi cantly diminishes problem-solving abilities and narrows rather than expands creative thinking.92 Seeing the glass half full, rather than half empty, is an aspiration of the good leader because of how it expands opportunities and possibilities, and spreads positive energy and motivation to others. Good leaders also know that emotions infl uence decision-making. Even though we like to believe we make decisions based on reason and logic, neuroscience has revealed that no one makes decisions based purely on logic alone. Our emotions infl uence our thoughts more than we oft en recognize, and logical reasoning is linked with emotional choices more than we like to admit.93 For leaders, this matters because the emotions of the leader will have an impact on decision-making, which is a central activity of leaders. Good leaders have a centred, balanced emotional nature that is generally positive and optimistic, enabling the leader to remain resilient despite challenges and have the self-confi dence to persevere.

## Even in undeniably negative situations, likeable leaders emanate an enthusiastic hope for the future, a confi dence that they can help make tomorrow better than today. Travis Bradberry

Aspiration #6: To Be Realistic and Thoughtfully Skeptical We have just explored why an optimistic outlook is such an essential part of good leadership. You may be wondering if this aspiration seems a contradiction of the previous one, and that is a reasonable question. However, healthy optimism is not a naïve denial of the facts or the inclination to ignore reasonable evidence to pursue one's own preferred course of action. Realistic optimism involves an optimistic and realistic view of the future—if there are good reasons to feel that the future will bode well.96 In contrast, unrealistic optimism can have very negative results, causing us to engage in behaviours or plans that will be to our detriment because we are not seriously considering the factors that can aff ect us.97 Th oughtful skepticism spurs us to look deeper, to ask hard questions, to explore beyond the surface. Realism causes us to consider what we have learned from the past and the world around us, to pay attention to patterns of cause and eff ect. Realism and thoughtful skepticism enhance optimism to ensure that decisions made will be prudent and wise, while also seizing on opportunities that others may not see. A good leader utilizes realistic optimism to acquire resources, to pursue goals, and to be persistent,98 with a realistic assessment of what can or cannot be achieved in a situation.99 However, unlike pessimism, this realistic and thoughtfully skeptical approach is balanced by positive perspective, emotions, and motivation.100 Aspiration #7: To be Dedicated and Committed Although it may seem rather obvious, it is worth noting that good leaders are dedicated and committed to their work, to their organizations, to the people they serve, and to the people who work for them. Th is strong sense of loyalty and support is part of what inspires loyal followership, and also translates into a strong sense of public service. Once again, it is worth repeating that those who work for government are servants—they are there to serve the public, not themselves, and to create mechanisms of excellence to ensure that service is provided in a way that will uphold the values and intentions of a government designed to take care of its people. Sadly, we hear too much about governments and political situations in which the public pays the price for self-serving government practices.

A good leader, guided by a strong ethical and moral compass, will not be blindly loyal to a system that needs to be changed. Th ere is a time and a place for speaking up, for questioning the status quo, and for indicating there is a better path. Good leaders not only encourage discussion and allow for diff erent perspectives, they also have the confi dence and integrity to speak up when needed. Healthy dedication to one's work involves dedication to principles, ideals and values that are part of that workplace, not blind loyalty when ethical missteps occur. Good leaders manage this delicate balance: demonstrating appropriate loyalty while also demonstrating moral courage and integrity.

Th e aspirations of a good leaderare guided by social responsibility and a strong moral compass. Th e good leader is strongly committed to a collaborative approach, aspiring to "get to yes" with others through a win-win approach. Th is is supported by the aspiration to motivate and affi rm others through an inspiring approach, with a strong commitment to excellence in every aspect of the organization. Th e good leader is optimistic, using a positive approach to motivate others and to see opportunities along with the challenges. Th is optimism is balanced with thoughtful skepticism, ensuring decisions are grounded in realism as well as the leader's vision. Th e good leader is dedicated to their team and devoted to their work, with a strong sense of loyalty and support for the organization as well as those who work for them. Th at sense of dedication is guided by their ethical and moral compass to ensure their loyalty and their integrity are not in confl ict.

# CHAPTER FOUR

# The Skills of a Good Leader

**Leaders can develop and cultivate skills to increase their success, but how they apply those skills will always be shaped by their inner values.**

In our earlier chapters we talked about the inner core, behaviours and aspirations of a good leader. As we have said before, who we are at the deepest part of ourselves will shape our behaviours and aspirations. Th at is why we continue to stress the importance of a strong inner core that will anchor the aspirations, behaviours, skills and commitments of a good leader. In this chapter, we will explore more deeply some of the specifi c skill areas that can be developed and cultivated to increase a leader's success. Clustering around the principled and ethical core, these skills shape how the leader communicates; how they handle confl ict; how they coach, mentor and evaluate personnel; how they build and lead teams; how they strategize and make decisions; and, how they manage practical operational realities such as fi nancial management and organizational tasks. It is worth considering once again that "doing" fl ows from "being." How we do things and how we apply our skills will always be shaped by our inner values and what we hold to be important. For that reason, we continue to put the strong inner core of the good leader in the centre of the circle. Th e skills we are going to discuss form the outer ring. Th ese skills cluster around three themes: communication skills, interpersonal skills, and the skills needed for strategic management, decision-making, and administration.

How Do Good Leaders Communicate? It is important to look at the overarching principles and behaviours associated with eff ective leadership through communication before we explore specifi c communication skill sets. It has been said that "knowledge is power." It is also true that withholding or misusing information can create climates of distrust, and problems for the leader. Transparency balanced with appropriate discretion and disclosure is a starting point. Successful leaders provide clear, consistent and continual communication among peers, employees, and stakeholders, whereas poor communication hinders relationships and can cause leader derailment.101 We are constantly communicating with each other through a variety of media; clear communication should be a fundamental component of the organization's culture.102 Th is includes sharing organizational vision and values up front and oft en, and supporting a culture of open interaction.103 Communication is also about receiving information, and the eff ective leader is a good listener. Th is requires openness, patience, and a willingness to encourage healthy debate, so that all views can be heard and explored.104 Respect, empathy, and a supportive approach enhance listening; asking clarifying questions and using good analytical skills will help the leader refi ne and use that information. It is especially important to create mechanisms to hear directly from the public and frontline service providers, as they oft en have direct experience and insights that can increase eff ectiveness and create cost effi ciencies. Th is conveys accountability and a servicefocused attitude.

***Good leaders know that not all confl ict is negative; often tension and differing perspectives can be leveraged to inspire creative solutions and collaboration.***

Eff ective leaders also recognize that not all confl ict is negative; oft en tension arising from diff ering perspectives can be leveraged to foster creative solutions and collaboration.105 Th e eff ective leader hears the other person's concerns, positions or demands; they also can discern and explore the underlying needs, interests and values driving those concerns, positions and demands. Th is enables them to build options that meet those underlying needs in mutually benefi cial ways.106 Fisher and Ury developed this collaborative problem-solving approach in their seminal book Getting to Yes. 107 Th eir approach to collaborative negotiation is discussed more deeply in Chapter Th ree: Aspirations. We have discussed the behaviours that fl ow from our inner selves: behaving ethically because we are guided by ethics, a moral framework, and a commitment to social responsibility. Th is includes treating others with respect and compassion because how we treat people matters. Good leaders also communicate eff ectively and listen to others because they value the contributions of those around them, and they strive to inspire others to uphold and follow the vision and values of the organization of which they are part. Th ese values-based behaviours provide an excellent foundation, and they are supplemented by task and skill-focused behaviours that enable the leader to ensure that goals are accomplished eff ectively and strategically.

Good leaders foster growing self-awareness and self-management to ensure that there is consistency and integrity between their inner core values and the way they function. Th is helps to ensure they are on a path of growth in how they handle their strengths, weaknesses, emotions, and behaviours.108 Building on a strong inner core and good communication, collaboration, and people skills, we will now look at the specifi c communication skills that are essential components of good leadership.

Skill #1: Verbal and Presentation Skills Th e ability to communicate eff ectively in a variety of settings is an essential skill for leaders. We have discussed already the importance of emotional intelligence, and the ability to interact with others in a way that is relational, supportive, and collaborative. Good leaders also make verbal presentations, write reports, prepare proposals and engage in a host of other tasks in which they need to communicate eff ectively. It is not only important to have the technical skills to communicate well, but to do so in a way that is inspirational and persuasive, so that others will engage with the leader's ideas around how to achieve big-picture organizational goals. What takes a presentation from the mundane to that magical place where people are moved to respond? Good leaders have cultivated a sense of rhetoric—a mastery of language that touches people at cognitive and emotional levels—creating a compelling eff ect. While some people have a natural inclination for this, it is a skill that can be learned. Many leaders have, on their own time, received training in eff ective, compelling public speaking. Th roughout history there have been powerful examples of individuals who have mastered this art of persuasion so eff ectively that their legacy lives on, long aft er their lives have ended. Th e great orators of the ages are part of this group. What made their speaking so powerful? What can good leaders learn from their example?

American civil rights activist Martin Luther King Jr. is an excellent example of an eff ective oral communicator. As a Baptist preacher he was well trained in how to deliver an eff ective sermon: it needed clear points, eff ective metaphors .and analogies, and eloquent, fl owing language that had a somewhat rhythmical, musical eff ect on the ears of those listening.

His 1963 speech "I have a dream" is an iconic example of his mastery of rhetoric. Very few of us can imagine ourselves being as infl uential and persuasive as Martin Luther King, but it is interesting to read or listen to his speech and note his repetition of key phrases, his use of powerful metaphors and word images, and the rising crescendo to his fi nal emphasis on freedom, repeated again and again. Repetition focuses the listener on the key ideas and drives them home, and King used this technique with extraordinary mastery.

## Inspiring others is the language of leadership.

Jay Conger from McGill University noted that inspiring others is the language of leadership. 109 According to Conger, eff ective leaders have the ability to skillfully craft the organization's mission, and to communicate that mission in ways that generate great intrinsic appeal. Th ese leaders can detect opportunities in their environment, and describe them in ways that maximize their signifi cance. Th ey can articulate an organization's mission and communicate it in ways that inspire. Inspiring leaders use stories and anecdotes that connect with the imaginations of their listeners, engaging them and fostering their interest; stories that convey the values and behaviours that are important to the organization. Th ey gear their language to their audience, and strategically use everyday language to communicate in down-to-earth ways. Th ey have mastered their tone of voice and body language to create a confi dent, credible and compelling presence. Former USA President Barak Obama and his wife Michelle both have this confi dent, down-to-earth communication style that is compelling, but enables them to be easily understood. Oprah Winfrey's acceptance speech for the Cecil B. De Mille Lifetime Achievement award at the 2018 Golden Globe Awards is an excellent example of masterful public speaking: not only was her content carefully knit together to create persuasive fl ow, but her delivery was dramatic, compelling and skillfully paced to ensure maximum impact on the emotions of the audience.

Skills and Techniques of Master Communicators What are the skills and techniques we can learn from these and other master communicators, if we want to improve our ability to make persuasive oral presentations?110 1. Frame the organization's mission around intrinsically appealing goals and draw upon values and beliefs that have positive, culturally-important meaning for your organization. Draw appealing links to the broader societal contributions of the organization and sincerely endorse and incorporate these. Th e leader's true beliefs in the organization's purpose are a cornerstone to becoming inspirational and are achieved only aft er signifi cant periods of exploration, refl ection, and eff ort. 2. In describing the organization's goals, incorporate the positive values that are deeply held by the organization and society at large. Use stories to illustrate these guiding values in action within the organization and the marketplace. 3. Highlight key belief categories when framing your description of the mission. Specifi cally, highlight the signifi cance of the mission, why it arose in the fi rst place, key antagonists, and assumptions about why it will succeed. 4. Employ more metaphors, analogies, and stories. Keep your message simple and focused. Repeat it consistently. 5. Experiment with various rhetorical techniques. Seek out coaches; get feedback. 6. Allow your emotions to surface as you speak. Are you excited about the vision and mission of your organization? If so, show it! Are you deeply concerned about competitive threats? Show it. Be mindful that persuasive public speaking can have a dark side. Adolf Hitler was a powerful communicator whose gift for persuasion brought about war, misery and loss of life for millions. History demonstrates that the persuasive oratory of a powerful leader can be co-opted for manipulative and coercive purposes, and this can play out in smaller ways in your organization just as it played out in larger ways in global confl ict. As ever, all our skills and aspirations need to be subordinated to our inner character, our ethics, and the principles and values that keep us from harming others or the world around us.

Skill #2: Written Communication Excellent leaders have also mastered other forms of communication, including the written word. Not every leader is gift ed with a talent for writing! Avail yourself of staff who can help you with editing, and who provide an extra set of eyes to spot typos, spelling mistakes and grammatical problems.111 It goes without saying that any document that will reach the public needs a robust proofreading and editing process, and wise leaders adopt a similar approach to any document of importance that will be landing on someone else's desk. Your standards for excellence should extend to how the written and spoken word are delivered. According to Th e Advisor, a resource for supervisors, managers and HR personnel, good leaders consider which form of communication will be most eff ective.112 Although email has become the quickest and easiest way to connect with others, wise leaders choose verbal communication for any message with emotional content, or with the potential for creating confusion on the part of the recipient.

Th e Advisor also suggests that announcements that will have a signifi cant impact on employees are best delivered in a meeting, and concerns about performance issues and other sensitive information are best handled one-to-one and privately. Written communication, including email, is oft en helpful in providing operational or technical instruction. In summary, tailor your message to your audience, keeping in mind their knowledge, expertise and experience. If your internal sense is causing you to feel cautious before you click "send" then ask a trusted colleague to look it over before you send it on.

Tips on Communicating Effectively Here are some more helpful tips from Th e Advisor on communicating eff ectively:113 1. Keep it simple. Use plain language to make your point, and use an economy of words. People receive a lot of information every day, so less is more. 2. Choose your words carefully. If you are upset, take a timeout before deciding how you will respond and which communication mechanism to use. If you will be speaking on a diffi cult subject, consider having talking points to guide you. 3. Be aware of body language and tone of voice. People react more to these than to the words you use. 4. Listen. Encourage the other person to do most of the talking. You will learn more and it builds rapport. You can gain a lot from casual, indirect conversations. 5. "Communicate, or else!" Withholding information creates an opportunity for employees to make up their own version of what is going on, and it will usually be incomplete or incorrect. Give as much information as is reasonable and appropriate. 6. Do not make promises you cannot keep. It may undermine your team's faith in you, and they may see you as a liar. "I don't know" or "I am unable to discuss it at this time" are fair responses if you cannot answer a question. 7. Solve problems. When someone presents a concern, listen carefully, ask questions, and discuss possible solutions. Th is sends the message that you are someone they can turn to when problems arise.

# CHAPTER FIVE

# The Communication Commitments of a Good Leader

**Communication is a key skill area for effective leaders. The ability to communicate well through a variety of mechanisms is part of the job.**

I n the last chapter we identifi ed the diff erence between aspirations, skills, and commitments. Once again, we should remember that commitments are the promises we make within ourselves to behave in a certain way over and over again. It is not something we aspire to do; it is something we commit to do. Aspirations stretch us and give us a goal to reach for; they help us expand our skills and abilities and continue our growth as leaders. Commitments refl ect our values and what is important to us, and what we are capable of doing right now on a daily basis. In this chapter we will look again at leaders and how they communicate, but with a specifi c focus on some key aspects of communication where leaders need to show consistency. Our fi rst two communication commitments begin within us, refl ecting our attitudes and values toward others and the spirit with which we interact with those around us. Commitment one relates to expressing gratitude and encouragement; commitment two involves cultivating open, transparent communication and workplace culture. Commitment three builds on the second commitment through the development of easy, accessible communication systems, and commitment four relates to the important practice of active listening, consultation, and the day-to-day behaviour of welcoming other perspectives in large-scale ways, and in one-to-one conversations. Our last commitment is specifi c to internal and external government stakeholders, to whom we commit to be open and transparent through eff ective information-sharing mechanisms. Communication, as we have seen over and over again, is a key skill area for eff ective leaders. Th e ability to communicate well through a variety of mechanisms is part of the job. Th is chapter identifi es important areas of communication where good leaders make promises within themselves to keep on doing something consistently, so that it becomes a natural and inherent part of the daily experience of working with that leader.As ever, our communication commitments are guided by our values and principles, so we continue to frame these commitments around that inner core of an ethical, principled moral compass.

Communication Commitment #1: Expressing Genuine Gratitude and Appreciation to Colleagues and Subordinates Expressing gratitude and appreciation are part of valuing our team members; this demonstrates that we not only appreciate them but want to encourage them as well. It may seem rather surprising that this has been placed at the top of the wheel, but here is why: appreciating, valuing, affi rming, thanking and encouraging colleagues and subordinates (and others) is harder than it looks as a daily practice. Not only that, it is strongly linked with the attributes of servant leadership which is a natural fi t for those in public service. What makes this so diffi cult? Why is it important that it becomes a daily commitment, and not just an aspiration? Th e tough answer is that we are human, and innately inclined to think fi rst about our own well-being, our own desires, our own goals and ambitions, and our own success. It is natural to pursue self-interest. It is much harder to think fi rst about the well-being of the team, and how others are doing around us. Th is is where it serves us well to refl ect deeply on what truly motivates us. Are we all about getting ahead, at the expense of others? How do others see us in this regard? Do they wonder if we are one of those "snakes in suits" who seem nice on the surface, but really can't be trusted?177 An attitude of gratitude and appreciation is more than just saying nice words to others at the appropriate moment. We are identifying something much deeper, something that connects to your inner core. It is about rising above the temptation to be ego-driven and self-serving, to focus on what people around you truly need, and on how you can be a source of ongoing support and encouragement to them. It is about doing something for others when there is nothing in it for you. But here is the interesting part: leaders who invest in their teams in this way usually receive the reward of loyalty and support from their team, who know their leader is their primary encourager and will not throw them under the bus.

What might this look like as it plays out on a daily basis? It means ensuring that people get the credit for the work they do—and not just to them directly, but in the presence of others as well. It means acknowledging with thanks when people are required to go above and beyond the regular requirements of the job. It means taking time to really get to know your people, and their hopes, dreams and goals, and helping them grow. It means saying in countless verbal and non-verbal ways, "I am so glad you are part of my team. What you do makes a positive diff erence here and I want you to know that I see it, and really appreciate it."

Valuing and appreciating people is another way of investing in them—there is power in acknowledgement and praise.178 When an employee believes his or her superiors are grateful for their work, the employee benefi ts by having an improved sense of worth within the organization, which can encourage ongoing performance improvements.179 Life is full of challenges, diffi culties and negative experiences. We oft en have no idea of the diffi cult things people are experiencing at work and in their personal lives, and frankly, it can suck the positive energy right out of them. When we can give meaningful encouragement and gratitude to others it oft en has the eff ect of giving water and fertilizer to a drooping, dry plant—it picks right up and begins to fl ourish again. We noted before the value of positive energy and optimism for workplace morale, and this connects with that idea. When we, as leaders, notice and affi rm all the good things our colleagues do and express our appreciation, thanks, and praise, it helps create a positive, encouraging environment. And it also helps to establish this behaviour as a cultural norm and positive example for others. We become a role model. Th ere is another interesting outcome of adopting a grateful attitude. Th is relates to the psychological reality that whatever we tend to focus on and dwell on becomes larger in our minds, and becomes a bigger and bigger part of our perspective. If we focus primarily on the negative, soon all we can see is the negative. If we cultivate a more positive, appreciative approach, and train ourselves to notice and acknowledge the things that are going well, we become better equipped to think in a more positive way. In an earlier chapter we noted the physical and psychological benefi ts of optimism and positivity—here is another setting in which we can cultivate it. Grateful people report higher levels of life satisfaction and optimism, and greater energy and connections with other people180—all of which will be positive within our organizations.

## If we train ourselves to notice the things that are going well, we become better equipped to think in a more positive way.

It takes daily practice to make this part of your working life, which is why we feel it needs to be one of your daily commitments. If this is a challenging area for you, start small and commit to acknowledging and appreciating at least one thing every day for which someone around you has been responsible. Continue to do this every day, and train yourself to become observant regarding the good things other people are doing, even the small things. Th en increase the numbers of times per day you can acknowledge the good things going on around you. Notice them. Acknowledge them. Show appreciation. Say thank you. Not only will you be a better person for doing it, you will have a happier team as a result.

Communication Commitment #2: Open, Transparent Communication We have noted previously the importance of a leader having integrity that inspires trust in followers. Nothing reduces trust quicker than the sense of being lied to, deceived, or having been manipulated in some way. Good leaders are committed to communicating truthfully and honestly, and with as much openness and transparency as can be permitted considering the confi dentiality requirements of the job. As we said earlier, knowledge is power. Furthermore, having and holding information puts a person in a position of power. For that reason, many leaders guard their information jealously, even when they do not need to be so vigilant. Good leaders are wise about how they handle information and when they release it. Th ey balance appropriate discretion with the realization that there is oft en benefi t in empowering the group through sharing information. As modern business structures become fl atter and less hierarchical, and collaboration and teamwork become more the norm, it challenges old paradigms about how we handle information and when we release it. Good leaders are prudent and wise in this regard, and they value openness and transparency. Th is is especially important in government settings, where there is the expectation of high accountability for how public resources are managed. Th e good news is that positive, transparent communication from leaders has been positively associated with higher degrees of trust in followers, with the added benefi t that followers perceive these leaders to be more eff ective.181 Th is is true not just in the good times, but even more so when an organization is undergoing change, downsizing, or dealing with other stressful experiences.

A positive approach combined with communication transparency was found to increase the willingness of followers to be vulnerable and place their trust in the leader during downsizing— which can be a common occurrence in government settings when cutbacks are happening. Transparency in this situation means that leaders demonstrate a pattern of openness and clarity in their behaviour toward others by sharing the information needed to make decisions, by accepting input from others, and by disclosing their personal values, motives and feelings in a way that enables followers to accurately assess leaders' competence and morality of actions. Transparency involves that crucial dimension of ethical behaviour in which actions and words align consistently. When a leader is transparent, followers can see what the leader values and stands for, and that the leader understands who they are as well.

Creating a Culture of Transparency Th ere are specifi c things leaders can do to operationalize their daily commitment to transparency and openness. Th e University of Florida Human Resource Services makes these suggestions to create a culture of transparency:183 • Show others that you care. People thrive when personal connections are forged and maintained. Relationship-building creates safety, understanding, appreciation and reliability. When employees feel seen, heard, affi rmed and supported, they are more likely to be loyal and supportive of the leader. • Be vulnerable. Most employees appreciate a leader who is genuine and authentic. Vulnerability demonstrates sincerity, and builds credibility. It does require maturity and judgment on the part of the leader to assess what to share, and how the employees will interpret and share it with others. One key area is to invite feedback on the leader's performance to discover how others perceive them. Th is demonstrates for employees that feedback is a powerful tool for improvement and for building a high performance team. • Be fi ercely honest. Be more transparent, especially on how decisions are made. Th is helps reduce the sense that there are hidden agendas at play. If you do not have all the pieces in place or are waiting on more data to come in—just say so. • Hold the tough conversations. Do not dance around performance issues. As already discussed, giving positive feedback and constructively critical feedback to promote improvement and growth is part of the leader's job. Employees need a workplace environment that does not tolerate bullying, uncivil interactions, unproductive gossiping, blaming of others, and negative behaviours that jeopardize the team's performance toward goals and objectives. A transparent leader makes sure that employees are clear that these tough conversations will happen when needed. • Pay attention to the mood in the offi ce. Listen, observe, and care about the experiences employees are having within the workplace. Let employees know that you are paying attention to these factors, and be mindful of your own moods—as we mentioned before, your own emotions can "infect" the team, both positively and negatively. • Keep your promises. Th is sets the tone for the entire organization, and builds trust. Show up on time for meetings, return emails promptly, and follow up on requests you have made of employees—these are examples of little things that build trust for bigger things. Communicate your promises cleanly and clearly to avoid any misunderstandings.

• Be composed. Leaders with self-control, poise, and patience minimize workplace anxiety and uncertainty. Employees are always watching their leaders, so stay strong and confi dent; smile oft en and authentically, and be compassionate. Th is helps neutralize workplace chaos and creates certainty that a confi dent, caring, fearless leader is in charge. • Deliver bad news well. Th is demonstrates courage, and shows you will do things for the good of the organization and the team. Bad news moves fast, so address it promptly with employees. Say as much as you can without divulging confi dences and do not play the blame game. When employees voice concerns or appear upset, listen to them so they feel you are "in it with them" and not throwing a mess on them and walking away. Let them know what the steps are to correct a situation and communicate oft en where you are in the process of handling the situation. According to the University of Florida Human Resource Services,184 when employees feel they work in a relational environment where there are no secrets, they are more connected and invested in the outcomes. Th is means no secrets about cash fl ow, hours worked, what to wear to work, how promotions are handled, goals and roadmaps, performance expectations, and the value each team member brings to the table. Transparency is something that is cultivated over time by repeated actions—it is not something you can do only once. You must remain consistent. It is not always easy and it can open leaders up to being wrong and being judged, but the benefi ts greatly outweigh the risks. Good leaders see the power of transparency and the positive impact it has on everything they do.

Communication Commitment #3: Accessible, Easy Communication Systems Building on the idea of openness and transparency, it is important for government leaders to advocate for technology and data systems that make it easy for the public to communicate and receive information from government offi ces. It is a common complaint that government websites and online application processes can be diffi cult to use, especially for those who, for a variety of reasons, may fi nd online systems challenging. Oft en those with personal challenges or vulnerabilities are those who need government help the most—therefore, it is important that communication systems work well for people of all capabilities. In an age of automation it can be frustrating for members of the public to face diffi culties in trying to talk with someone, especially if there are complicated telephone menus, chronic busy signals, or long hold times.

Communication Commitment #4: Welcoming Other Perspectives through Consultation and Active Listening In our earlier chapters we identifi ed the importance of a collaborative approach. We also suggested developing a communication style that is supported by active listening. We need to remind ourselves what active listening is, so we can think about how oft en during each day we are using this important skill. Active listening is more than refraining from speaking when others are talking—it involves thinking deeply about what the other person is saying, asking open, probing questions to get more information and greater understanding, and using communication skills such as paraphrasing, summarizing, clarifying, and reframing. Active listening involves talking, but from the perspective that you are focused on trying to deepen your understanding of the other person's perspective. It is not about advancing your own view or debating the subject.

Active listening involves curiosity and openness to explore how other people see things. It involves showing empathy toward what they feel. It enables you to explore the deeper levels of needs, fears, interests, beliefs and values, which are oft en not expressed until someone asks about them. It also involves moments of silence as you allow the other person to continue to sort out what they are thinking and feeling. While active listening can happen in one-to-one conversations or meetings, many levels of government and government departments are adopting active listening through larger processes of community engagement and consultation, realizing that it is vital for governments to understand the issues and concerns of communities and individuals who live there. It is diffi cult to make signifi cant decisions within a community without support and buy-in. Th erefore, governments are increasingly appreciating that they need to solicit information from local stakeholders, individuals, community groups, and others before making decisions that will aff ect the daily lives of their constituents. Processes of consultation and active listening will inevitably bring up areas of disagreement and dissent. People naturally see situations diff erently, and their perspectives are shaped by their experiences and personal knowledge. Good leaders are not intimidated by this—they expect it. It is not seen as a threat, but as a natural part of exploring what is needed to create healthy, vibrant and fl ourishing communities. Good leaders commit themselves to active listening regularly, and to consultation processes when decisions are made that will have an impact on the lives of others. A good leader will always welcome other perspectives, knowing that in the diversity of ideas and opinions there may be the creative beginnings of a workable solution or outcome for the problems at hand.

## Feedback is a gift. Ideas are the currency of our next success. Let people see you value both feedback and ideas

Communication Commitment #5: Information-sharing with Stakeholders, and Being Committed to Building the Necessary Information Systems to Facilitate It Th is commitment is strongly related to the previous commitment because it involves many of the same issues and values, although they may be addressed through a diff erent approach. Stakeholders are group of people with a strong and particular interest in what the government is doing, because it has an impact on their work, the clients they serve, or on their daily life. Stakeholders may be internal or external to government, but they are all aff ected in some way by the government's actions, objectives, products, services, or policies. While Commitment #5 and Commitment #4 are similar, stakeholder information-sharing will oft en involve developing positive, informal relationships as well as more formalized processes of giving and receiving information. Good leadership in government promotes strong and healthy relationships with stakeholders. Deloitte & Touche recommend that organizations formalize the implementation of a formal stakeholder engagement policy.188 Not only will this enhance the value of the stakeholder engagement process, but it will also reduce the risk of missing important perspectives, which may cause embarrassment or negatively aff ect the reputation of the government department in question. According to Deloitte & Touche, the stakeholder engagement process and policy approach usually involves the following steps:189 • Defi ne the scope of the policy • Defi ne the ownership and decision-making process • Defi ne the governance process • Identify the key stakeholders and stakeholder groups, given their infl uence and dependence on the organization • Develop an engagement plan, including frequency, method and channel • Facilitate the stakeholder engagement process • Identify the legitimate concerns and interests of key stakeholders • Design a process for dealing with confl icts between stakeholder concerns • Defi ne a mechanism to feed stakeholder concerns into strategic planning to ensure alignment

Provide feedback to stakeholder groups • Generate reports, including input for an Integrated Report for key stakeholdersWhile this may seem rather mechanical, the process is a logical sequence of steps that will ensure that mechanisms are in place to invite input, gather information regarding needs, interests, and concerns of stakeholders, and have a way of processing and communicating that information in strategic ways. All levels of government encounter community concerns that relate to public safety, and the desire for prosperity and human thriving. It is diffi cult to address these concerns eff ectively without appreciating the perspectives of those who will be directly aff ected, which is why community consultation and engagement is growing in importance. Information-sharing with stakeholders may also involve improved access to technology, particularly online information systems that help improve two-way communication between government and the public. Th ese mechanisms are tools to bring to life the leadership commitment to be open, inclusive, and welcoming of other perspectives. Th is helps reduce the "fortress mentality" that oft en keeps government departments from engaging the public eff ectively. It also helps reduce a sense of "we know better than they do," which can keep government departments advancing policy that is not understood or supported at the community level.

*A commitment to be open and welcoming of other perspectives helps reduce the "fortress mentality" that often keeps governments from engaging the public effectively.*

Summary

Communication commitments are embraced and practised daily by good leaders, demonstrating their willingness to be open, transparent, and concerned about others. Th is expresses itself through caring behaviours such as active listening; encouraging, thanking and praising others; inviting input; and building mechanisms and processes to ensure that information can fl ow easily to the people who need it. Communication commitments also ensure we are able to receive information from our stakeholders. Specifi cally, our communication commitments begin fi rst with a daily practice of appreciating, acknowledging and expressing gratitude to those around us and to those who work for us. Th is fosters a positive, encouraging work environment with more highly engaged employees.

Our second commitment is to open, transparent communication with our teams and others, followed by a third commitment to open, accessible communication systems for those inside and outside the organization. Th ese are enhanced by our fourth commitment to active listening, to consultation, and to welcoming other perspectives. Commitment four is expressed in onto-one conversations and meetings, and includes much larger consultation processes, which demonstrate the value we place on hearing the perspectives of others. Finally, commitment fi ve is targeted specifi cally toward information-sharing with government stakeholders, who are in a unique relationship with us.

Good leaders are committed to: 1. formally and informally expressing sincere gratitude and appreciation to colleagues and subordinates for work well done 2. open and transparent communication 3. easy and accessible communication (for example, user-friendly technology and data systems) 4. encouraging input—including criticism and critical perspectives—through active listening, consultation, and being consistently inclusive 5. improving information-sharing and information systems with relevant stakeholders

# CHAPTER SIX

# The Sustainability Commitments of a Good Leader

*Because leaders in unique positions to provide visionary leadership that is responsible, sustainable, and innovative.*

I n the previous two chapters we discussed a variety of commitments related to information and communications. In this chapter we want to be forward-thinking, considering the long-term health and sustainability of our organizations, and the health and wellness of the people who work for and with us. Sustainability is a popular term: every company, business, NGO and branch of government seems to be considering how to become more sustainable. But what does sustainability mean for those who work in government? One aspect of it certainly relates to environmental concerns and social responsibility. But organizational sustainability also supports healthy workplaces with good retention and succession planning, and highly engaged, committed employees who are fl ourishing within an organizational culture of support and respect. Sustainability also connects to ideas of innovation, growth, and continuous development and improvement. In the business world, this is vital—and can make the diff erence between surviving or shutting the doors. However, the nature of government is such that bureaucracies can survive even when they are ineffi cient and lacking in innovation, or when the workforce is not happy but is inclined to stay because of job security, generous salaries or benefi t plans. Th erefore, good leaders in government need to go further to ensure that sustainability includes the health and well-being of employees and the workplace culture. In one sense, governments—not business—should be on the leading edge of sustainability that is socially, fi scally, and environmentally responsible because of their obligation to serve the public, and what is owed to the taxpayer. Th ey do not have the temptation of making a profi t at the expense of principle. Governments exist to provide structure, governance, safety and help, and to provide leadership in ways that improve the quality of life for all without causing further harm. Th ey are not, and should not become, self-serving organizations. Th erefore, leaders in various levels of government are in unique positions to provide visionary leadership that is responsible, sustainable, and innovative.

From the perspective of business, sustainability is about demonstrating social responsibility by balancing business results with concern for the greater good.190 Although corporations are paying more and more attention to environmental issues, the notions of sustainability and social responsibility both look beyond short-term results to long-term implications of decisions and how they aff ect health, safety, the environment, and other areas of concern.191 It means embedding social responsibility into processes and procedures, and taking responsibility for the impact that decisions will have on the workplace.192 Is government really that diff erent? Th e concerns are similar, and good leaders must consider the intended and unintended consequences of decisions and how they infl uence the workforce, the environment, and overall operations. Th ere should be a similar desire to balance results with concern for the greater good. As expressed by the Cambridge Program for Sustainable Leadership, "a sustainable leader is someone who inspires and supports action towards a better world."193 In our understanding of holistic, organizational sustainability we see it through two diff erent lenses: human and operational. Human sustainability involves a commitment to employee health and well-being. It means daily commitments to develop an engaged, committed workforce with a high level of employee satisfaction. Achieving this means a commitment to respect, and fostering a work environment that affi rms dignity and respect daily. Human sustainability requires us to look ahead to the long-term welfare of the organization, with a commitment to succession planning. Th is involves ensuring that young or emerging leaders are supported to learn and grow, so that they will be well-equipped to move into higher positions of responsibility as others move on. It means ensuring that people receive the training they need when they need it. Human sustainability also involves a daily commitment to nurturing positive relationships throughout the organization, for internal and external stakeholders as well as your employees. Operational sustainability is more institutional in focus. It demonstrates a commitment to the serious review of suggestions for innovation or change. It is a commitment to a system of continuous improvement, guided by a desire for quality and excellence. Th ese are achieved through commitments to ongoing assessment, cross-comparison assessment, and built-in mechanisms for evaluation, as part of a larger commitment to strive for best practices. Operational sustainability also looks outward, through careful consideration of the institutional brand or corporate image. Commitments in this area keep a good leader working to strengthen how their organization is perceived by the public. Finally, operational sustainability commitments involve forward-thinking fi scal and environmental responsibility.

## *A sustainable leader is someone who inspires and supports action towards a better world*

Human Sustainability To be successful, we need to look deeper at the people-oriented, human sustainability commitments that are linked with good leadership. Obviously, it is diffi cult to sustain the work of an organization if there is low morale, rapid turnover and transience, or if there are entrenched negative attitudes or behaviours that aff ect productivity and success. Th is is why we assert that good leaders' sustainability commitments must be more than environmental. Th ey must address the very essence and nature of the workplace itself. As we have noted before, good leaders set a tone by their words and actions—they are role models and they chart the path for others. However, it is not enough simply to model the behaviours one wants to see in others. Good leaders take steps regularly to ensure high job satisfaction as well as high productivity and engagement in the workforce. Sustainability Commitment #1: Employee Job Satisfaction Job satisfaction is positively associated with a high level of commitment on the part of the employee toward the organization. Researchers have noted that highly committed workers have a strong belief in, and acceptance of, the organization's goals and values. Th ey personally identify with the organization. Th ey have a willingness to exert a considerable eff ort on the part of the organization, and they have a strong intent or desire to remain with the organization. Th ey are loyal.195 When commitment fl ows from the worker to the organization, the organization benefi ts. But what does the organization need to do to create a working experience that produces this level of loyalty and commitment? Some things are obvious, like appropriate compensation, benefi ts and advancement opportunities.

However, job satisfaction goes deeper than that. It involves an emotional attachment and connection to the workplace. It is aff ected by relations with colleagues and superiors, and how employees perceive the workplace culture and their own performance within it.196 It is also linked with the behaviour of their leaders. Research fi ndings indicate that employees who perceive their superiors as adopting consultative or participative leadership behaviour are more committed to their organizations, more satisfi ed with their jobs, and score higher in their performance.197 Eff ective leaders are considered by employees to be fl exible, off ering guidance to employees, yet allowing them to show initiative and be creative.198 Th is is consistent with what we have noted about the importance of being collaborative, listening to your team, sharing information, empowering your workers, and consulting with others. Daily commitments for a sustainable work force need to include an inner commitment to these values and practices. Sustainability Commitment #2: Employee Health and Wellness Human sustainability is linked with the ongoing promotion of employee health and wellness. Ensuring health and safety issues are addressed, plus building a wellness culture, can be part of what sustains organizational life. Even though workers spend many hours per week at their place of employment, their lives are much more complex and multi-dimensional. Emotional stresses, fi nancial pressures, or poor health or lifestyle choices may all aff ect how they perform at work. Ill health costs employers, and preventable health problems are not in the employee's or the employer's best interests. Th erefore, more and more workplaces are recognizing that promoting overall health, fi tness and good nutrition, and other wellness strategies, pays longrun dividends. A healthier workforce will typically be more productive and will generally be happier. Promoting wellness means promoting a lifestyle in which the needs of mind, body and spirit are addressed, and in which mental health and physical health are both important. As always, leaders are role models and provide an example to the rest of the team. Th ey can play an integral role in ensuring that wellness is encouraged on a daily basis, and this includes allocating time, money and resources to ensuring that wellness becomes part of the organization's daily life.

Sustainability Commitment #3: Cultures of Respect As we have just discussed, having healthy, satisfi ed, and positively engaged workers is part of organizational sustainability. Good leaders not only foster this, but also commit to creating an environment where preserving dignity and maintaining respect are the norm. Sutton's book, Good Boss, Bad Boss, points out that the best bosses balance performance and humanity, getting things done in ways that enhance rather than undermine dignity and pride.199 In Sutton's view, bosses ought to be judged by what they and their people accomplish, and by how their followers feel along the way.200 Good leaders want their workers to feel a sense of pride and dignity; they actively foster a climate of mutual respect that supports the ongoing quest for excellence and high performance. It is diffi cult to sustain your workforce if people feel angry, disrespected or mistreated. Good leaders do all they can to foster positive working environments where people feel valued, respected and listened to, and where they have a sense of pride and accomplishment about what they do. Sustainability Commitment #4: Staff Development, Training, and Succession Planning Th e next commitment that specifi cally relates to leading and supporting one's team or subordinates includes a commitment to staff development, training, and succession planning. Part of empowering people is to ensure they have access to ongoing growth and development opportunities. Th is not only validates them and supports improved performance, but it helps create ongoing renewal and growth so that renewal can be managed with greater ease. Good leaders are concerned about fostering this kind of renewal by investing in young or emerging leaders, ensuring they have the mentoring and support they need to take on new responsibilities and move into higher levels of leadership and responsibility as opportunities arise. If some employees are an obvious wrong fi t for the job, the good leader is already engaged in the ongoing performance review process to help re-direct them, or ultimately, to help them move on to something else that is a better fi t for them. Sustainability commitments involve ensuring that you have the right people for the job—and that you provide them the training and support to ensure they continue to function that way.

Sustainability Commitment #5: Internal and External Stakeholder Relationships Our last human sustainability commitment looks beyond the workers to internal and external stakeholders, without whose support it can be very diffi cult to accomplish our goals. Good leaders are committed to building positive relationships with their internal and external stakeholders, and they cultivate these relationships regularly. As we have asserted, having a collaborative approach is key. Valuing others and their input, working together in cooperative ways, being open to other points of view—all are part of maintaining positive relationships. Th is can be diffi cult in a government setting, where stakeholders may hold confl icting or divergent views, with diff erent claims on government time, energy and resources. However, responsible leadership includes proactive and inclusive engagement with stakeholders, and the promotion and facilitation of inclusive dialogue and discourse that will help guide ethically sound decision-making.201 Responsible business leaders have to deal with the moral complexity that results from a multitude of stakeholder claims, and they recognize the need to build enduring and mutually benefi cial relationships with all relevant stakeholders.202 Government leaders have the same challenge and responsibility. Building these benefi cial relationships with stakeholders is understood as a signifi cant component of building social capital, the various networks of relationships which can work together for collective good. Social capital consists of "the stock of active connections among people: the trust, mutual understanding, and shared values and behaviours that bind the members of human networks and communities and make cooperative action possible."203 What matters, according to the principles of corporate and social responsibility, is that leaders make sure that their organizations adopt a truly inclusive and ethically sound way of creating value for all legitimate stakeholders, even those who may have been previously excluded; it also includes future generations.

### *Responsible leadership includes proactive and inclusive engagement with stakeholders, and the promotion of dialogue that will help guide ethically sound decision-making.*

In summary, good leaders are committed to human sustainability. Th ey work regularly to ensure the workplace is grounded in dignity and respect, and they encourage employee wellness, learning and growth. Th ey are concerned about employee job satisfaction, and foster employee commitment through a variety of strategies, including the provision of training, professional development, and opportunities for growth and advancement. Th ey think ahead and plan for transition and change with eff ective succession planning. Taking the broader view, they ensure that stakeholder relationships are positive, within and outside the organization, creating healthy networks of relationships that can be used to achieve common goals and objectives. Th ey take the long view, with a commitment to building a healthy future for current stakeholders and future generations.

Operational Sustainability Operational sustainability is also important for good leaders. Here you see the practices and values that people most oft en associate with the idea of sustainability. Th is includes social and environmental responsibility, and the commitment to make decisions in ways that support the common good. It also requires commitments to key practices within the organization to ensure these larger goals are met. Th ese include the commitment to considering and reviewing suggestions for innovation and change. It involves a commitment to a system of continuous improvement, because good leaders value excellence and quality in services and products. Continuous improvement is supported by commitments to ongoing assessment and evaluation, cross-comparison assessments, and a desire to determine and implement best practices. It also includes a commitment to be future-focused, with strong fiscal responsibility.

Sustainability Commitments #6 & 7: Continuous Improvement Through Monitoring, Assessment, and Evaluation We have already discussed the importance of building in mechanisms for ongoing evaluation and review, to ensure that programs are delivering what they are designed to accomplish. Operational sustainability commitments include a commitment to monitoring programs and activities. Is the program on track to meet its expected outcomes? Th is involves knowing where the program started (identifying a baseline), having a sense of comparison with what other similar programs achieve (positing benchmarks), and having a clear sense of what is to be achieved (identifying targets).205 Cross-comparison analysis also enables the leader to compare similar programs from diff erent jurisdictions, to help determine how well their own program is faring in comparison with others. How are these cross-comparisons helpful? Even if a government program or initiative appears to be effi cient or eff ective, sometimes examining an alternative way of accomplishing the ultimate objective will reveal a better way. Good leaders are always open to new and better ways to increase effi ciency, eff ectiveness, and overall program success. Th e commitment to continuous improvement will compel the good leader to ensure that mechanisms are in place to conduct this sort of ongoing evaluation, with the willingness to consider new or diff erent approaches if change is needed.

Sustainability Commitment #8: Innovation As we discussed in earlier chapters, good leaders strive for innovation and aspire to foster creativity and new ways of thinking. Here, we examine the daily commitments that help the leader ensure that creativity and innovation become an integral part of organizational life. It begins with the leader's commitment to promoting and acknowledging the creative process. Th is can be diffi cult, because there are oft en points of tension between traditional business thinking and innovative, creative thinking. Both approaches are valid—it is a question of when to use each for best results

Good leaders know that sometimes it helps to depart from the tried-and-true paths. Part of being a visionary leader is to imagine a desired future state and how to get there; however, doing that without creativity and innovation can be extremely diffi cult. While we support the commitment to evidence-based practice and data-driven decision making, we also recognize that there are times when it helps to adopt a curiosity-driven, exploratory, and more imaginative approach to problem-solving.

It means striving for a better way, and it involves the willingness to explore multiple possibilities. Ambiguity then becomes an advantage, not a problem. It allows us to ask, "What if?"207 Operational sustainability then means committing oneself to using an evidence-based approach to assess and evaluate processes and programs, while also embracing creativity and innovation as a way of bringing about growth and improvement. Good leaders balance traditional business thinking (with its emphasis on evidence, evaluation and assessment) with innovation thinking, which encourages collaboration, team thinking, and exploration of "outside-the-box" ideas. Sustainable organizations need an appropriate balance of both to ensure they can meet and surmount challenges or unexpected threats. Furthermore, a culture of innovation allows ideas to grow and fl ourish, adds value, and helps the organization meet its targets.208 Good leaders foster creativity, but also have the skill to determine which ideas to support and to develop the appropriate mechanisms to ensure the execution of a new idea will be successful. For many leaders, this means developing their ability to release the intelligence, creativity and initiative of people throughout the organization, and then to integrate new initiatives toward an agreed vision of the future and solving whatever problems are encountered along the way.209 Sustainability Commitment #9: Consultation and the Corporate

"Brand" Leadership requires an ongoing commitment to evaluation, to assess how well the organization is doing to meet its goals and targets, and how well the organization is supporting internal, healthy workplace practices while also thinking about its public face. Every organization or business needs to think about its image or its "brand." Th e same commitment to evaluation that causes good leaders to use data and other evidence to assess eff ectiveness will inspire the leader to think about the public's perception and opinion of the organization, and what might be needed to address any defi cits. Th e communication commitment to public engagement and consultation can work well with this commitment to strengthening the corporate brand or image. When government organizations engage in meaningful stakeholder engagement and consultation, it not only strengthens the image or brand, but it can also stimulate an increased sense of pride and respect for the organization in the eyes of the employees. It must be noted, though, that consultation must be sincere and meaningful, motivated by a genuine desire to increase understanding and be inclusive. It must not be ritualistic.

Employees and the public will lose respect for leaders who waste one another's time through consultation processes that are mainly for show, when the course of action has already been decided. It is not ethical or responsible to mislead people in this way simply to keep up appearances or look good in the public eye. On the other hand, when there is genuine consultation and the results will help shape the fi nal outcome, respect for government is usually increased among employees and internal and external stakeholders.

Sustainability Commitment #10: Forward-thinking Fiscal Responsibility Sustainability leadership also involves fi scal responsibility. Leaders are stewards of resources that are human, material, fi nancial, and environmental. Governments are frequently criticized for how they allocate funds, and how spending is either too much (creating defi cits) or too little, thereby under-resourcing programs and initiatives intended for the public good. Political pressure in a time of restraint can create silo-based thinking, where each department or ministry is rewarded by how they trim and cut back — whereas fi scal responsibility might be better served by looking broadly across many departments and thinking about how savings can be achieved laterally, not just in isolated departments. Furthermore, small strategic investments can sometimes result in signifi cant returns. For example, within the realm of healthcare, certain drugs are relatively inexpensive to produce and sell, and it may seem to be in the government's best interest to encourage the use of these drugs to keep health costs down. Th ere are, however, examples of how this thinking can backfi re, producing the opposite eff ect than intended. Warfarin is an example of a drug that has been long on the market and is less expensive to purchase than newer blood thinners. It is not surprising that this would be a preferred option when the government is paying for an individual's drug plan. However, Warfarin is highly toxic—it was originally developed as rat poison and kills rodents by causing massive internal haemorrhage.

### *frequently criticized for how they allocate funds, and how spending is either too much or too little.*

When a test was developed to help monitor its eff ects on the human bloodstream, it became possible to use Warfarin as an anti-coagulant. However, because of its toxicity, it requires frequent blood testing to ensure the patient is staying healthy while using the drug. Th is represents ongoing additional costs to the health care system, because the patient is required to be monitored regularly by a physician and through regular lab tests. However, if the physician and lab costs are paid by a diff erent department than the one that pays for the drug plan, these costs will not be immediately apparent. Each department will believe they are operating within good budget parameters. A broader view—and a more ethical one—would be to compare the costs for both departments with the cost of using a newer, less toxic drug that does not have such potentially harmful side eff ects or require such rigorous follow-up. It would be a healthier option for the patient and it would decrease overall costs, while recognizing the initial cost would be higher to purchase the alternate medication. Another important example of fi scal sustainability relates to infrastructure spending. While governments are bound by four-year election cycles it can be tempting to avoid tackling the big projects that will bring benefi ts to the taxpayers for years and years to come. However, taking the shorter view can decrease safety, and increase environmental problems. Delaying the work may mean it becomes more expensive later when the project is fi nally started. Th is is also true in public safety. Placing a low priority on crime prevention and street-level social problems can result in higher costs for emergency responders, fi re services, police, and hospitals.210 Again, sustainable leadership looks at the long-term implications of providing (or not providing) services, as well as the immediate needs. Good leaders have the courage to take the long view. Sustainable leadership is complex. It involves both human and operational commitments. It is also values-based, and is aspirational in nature. When assessing the success of certain educational institutions over others, the Spencer Foundation examined organizational change over 30 years in eight diff erent Canadian and American schools. A researcher's examination of their study provides seven principles of sustainable leadership, listed on the next page. While the fi rst is specifi c to education, the rest are relevant for other government leaders as well.

Seven Principles of Sustainable Leadership

1. Sustainable leadership creates and preserves learning that will be ongoing and sustaining. 2. Sustainable leadership secures success over time, achieved through succession planning and succession management. 3. Sustainable leadership sustains the leadership of others, through distributing leadership opportunities and grooming successors. 4. Sustainable leadership addresses issues of social justice; it recognizes that one's own actions have an eff ect on the wider environment. 5. Sustainable leadership develops rather than depletes human and material resources. It is thrift y without being cheap; it carefully manages resources while taking care of people and helping them to take care of themselves. 6. Sustainable leadership develops environmental diversity and capacity. Promoters of sustainability cultivate a working environment that has the capacity to stimulate continuous improvement on a broad front. Th ey enable people to adapt to and prosper in their increasingly complex environment by learning from one another's diverse practices. 7. Sustainable leadership undertakes activist engagement with the environment. Th is may mean intensive engagement with stakeholders, creating strategic alliances and forging the connections necessary to make the changes that are needed to protect our environmental futures.

Summary

In conclusion, the sustainability commitments that are part of the BASICS of good leadership encompass human and operational concerns. On the human level they foster healthy workplaces of dignity and respect, where highly engaged and productive workers experience job satisfaction, and ongoing growth and development. Upcoming leaders are groomed and trained to ensure organizational growth and succession management. Training and professional development support continuous improvement, which is also supported by evaluation, assessment, and creative innovation where needed. Sustainability commitments look outward to stakeholder relationships, and how those outside the organization perceive it. Social capital is built through strong networks of mutually respectful and benefi cial stakeholder relationships, and eff ort is given to managing the organizational identity and brand.

Sustainability commitments also involve fi scal and environmental responsibility, with an understanding that social responsibility and social justice are inherent to the success of government in the eyes of stakeholders, the wider community and society at large. Th is requires appropriate stewardship of resources, eff ective timelines for projects, evidence-based evaluation, and a commitment to environmental responsibility.

Good leaders demonstrate they are committed to: HUMAN SUSTAINABILITY 1. a high degree of employee job satisfaction 2. employee health and wellness 3. building an organizational culture of respect 4. staff development and training (including succession planning) 5. developing and maintaining constructive, mutually beneficial, and positive relationships with both internal and external stakeholders OPERATIONAL SUSTAINABILITY 1. a system of continuous improvement 2. ongoing assessment, cross-comparison assessment, and evaluation towards best practice 3. placing value on suggestions for innovation / change 4. strengthening an institutional brand / corporate image 5. forward-thinking fiscal responsibility

# CHAPTER SEVEN

# A Last Look in the Mirror

*Find a way to nurture your inner core, your moral compass that will guide your path. For many, this is not just an intellectual exercise; it is akin to a spiritual journey.*

As we noted at the beginning of this book, not everyone can be a great leader. But we can all aspire to be good leaders, and take the steps necessary to become one. We are all heir to human fallibility and the inevitable mistakes and growing pains that are part of continuous improvement. However, we can still make the commitment to aspire to be a leader who will refl ect what we have explored here. Our world is desperate for good leadership. More than that, the workings of government rely on the principled, ethical values of leaders, who lead their teams and departments with the behaviours, aspirations, skills, and commitments that refl ect a strong inner core of good character. Th is is an essential part of the larger picture of being a visionary, results-oriented, people-focused and caring leader who communicates skillfully and leads strategically with innovation, courage, and a focus on sustainability. For some, developing the inner core of a good leader will be the hardest part. We encourage you to take steps to learn more about what it means to be ethical, principled, and socially responsible in the setting where you work. Find a way to nurture your inner core, your moral compass that will guide your path. For many, this is not just an intellectual exercise; it is akin to a spiritual journey. Th ere is oft en a transcendent aspect to the inner core of good leaders who are truly transformational in their workplaces. Find out about that, do some digging and exploration to discover what that is truly about. We encourage you to never stop nurturing your inner core, because life will never stop bringing circumstances that will challenge it. Perhaps it is time for some further self-refl ection. Maybe you have come to see that there are areas of your leadership that need more attention. We encourage you to explore the tools that will help you get there.

In thinking about that, you always need to have in mind that people around will almost never give you direct criticism about yourself. Th is is even truer when they really respect and like you. Th ey will think it, they will tell others, but they will not tell you. Th at is why you have to be very mindful and proactive about self-improvement. 360 Tools Using a 360 tool is an eff ective way to discern how you and others are perceived as leaders. Th e management consulting fi eld off ers many variations on these tools. Most commonly, they are basic questionnaires designed and administered to obtain anonymous feedback from employees and other relevant stakeholders on co-workers, supervisors, and managers in an organization. Th e questionnaire will usually provide a listing of leadership or work characteristics deemed to be important. In considering each characteristic, the person completing it will check a box or otherwise assign a score to indicate the extent to which they believe the individual being assessed demonstrates a particular trait. Th e collective responses from all of those completing the questionnaire are then presented to the person being assessed. Th is presentation will normally be done in concert with a discussion about how the individual assessed themselves, using the same tool. Accordingly, the person being assessed will have the opportunity to see how their self-perception fi ts with the view others have of them. It not only provides an opportunity to identify strengths, it will also call attention to those characteristics that the individual being assessed should improve upon. A 360 tool can be enormously helpful in enabling employees and others to provide both positive and constructive critical feedback in a non-threatening way. But it has to be done right.213 Th ese tools are only appropriate when you have enough people completing them so no one participant can be identifi ed, and when the participants have enough experience and knowledge to make a fair assessment of characteristics being considered. In the end, it is important to remember that we cannot become what we need to be, by remaining what we are.

360 Tools Using a 360 tool is an eff ective way to discern how you and others are perceived as leaders. Th e management consulting fi eld off ers many variations on these tools. Most commonly, they are basic questionnaires designed and administered to obtain anonymous feedback

from employees and other relevant stakeholders on co-workers, supervisors, and managers in an organization. Th e questionnaire will usually provide a listing of leadership or work characteristics deemed to be important. In considering each characteristic, the person completing it will check a box or otherwise assign a score to indicate the extent to which they believe the individual being assessed demonstrates a particular trait. Th e collective responses from all of those completing the questionnaire are then presented to the person being assessed. Th is presentation will normally be done in concert with a discussion about how the individual assessed themselves, using the same tool. Accordingly, the person being assessed will have the opportunity to see how their self-perception fi ts with the view others have of them. It not only provides an opportunity to identify strengths, it will also call attention to those characteristics that the individual being assessed should improve upon. A 360 tool can be enormously helpful in enabling employees and others to provide both positive and constructive critical feedback in a non-threatening way. But it has to be done right.213 Th ese tools are only appropriate when you have enough people completing them so no one participant can be identifi ed, and when the participants have enough experience and knowledge to make a fair assessment of characteristics being considered.

Th ey are not a mechanism for people to hide behind anonymity to say things that are unkind or cruel, or to backstab a colleague to help themselves get ahead. Similarly, the process needs to be protected from collusion, where workers may develop coalitions in the spirit of "you scratch my back and I'll scratch yours."214 A 360 tool is only a snapshot at one moment in time, and it needs to be included within a wider array of strategies for support, development and evaluation. It also has to be quick and easy to complete and easy to administer. Further, it is critical that the administrator/facilitator be especially skilled in delivering and discussing feedback in a developmental way. Otherwise, the process can be intimidating and demoralizing. It is also important to avoid the practice of using these tools only when things are going badly or when an employee's performance is suff ering. Too oft en, supervisors do not affi rm the positives when things are going well, and performance review processes can be neglected in the years when there are no concerns. It is not fair to use them as a mechanism to trigger a dismissal, or to neglect ongoing and continuous support and feedback that should be taking place on a regular basis. It is also wise to avoid using them as part of a promotion process or to determine compensation.215 "I've seen departments blow up and employees leave companies because the 360 wasn't handled properly... 360s are most eff ective when they are used as a development tool, not a rating tool." 216 (Leadership coach Alicia Arenas) Despite these cautions, there are numerous reasons to use 360 tools if you want to develop your strengths and give attention to the areas that need development. To help you develop the BASICS of good leadership, we invite you to review the 360 tool in the Appendix that is based on the leadership characteristics discussed in this book. You may fi nd it a helpful option in consideration of other 360 tools available in the marketplace. At the same time, you need to have in mind "what's next" aft er the administration of a 360 or feedback in any other form. Th at is where coaching and mentoring become all important. It is also where education and training are commonly helpful. A 360 tool can be a useful complement to other strategies that support learning and growth, and can assist leaders in developing self-awareness and reducing their blind spots. As stated, they must be administered appropriately and presented to the individual being assessed in a way that fosters growth and development, instead of diminishing their morale.

Educating and Developing Leaders It is worth noting that researchers, when trying to determine what good leadership is all about, usually end up learning a lot more about ineff ective and poor leadership. As we said in the opening chapter of this book, poor leadership abounds. Nearly everyone can think of personal examples of when they have been subjected to ineff ective or even damaging leadership. As this book concludes, we need to remind ourselves of some of the pitfalls you will want to avoid. A 2009 study from the University of Leicester concluded that ineff ective leaders are not trusted; they operate with questionable integrity; they fail to consult others while leading; and, they ignore problems.217 Th ose ineff ective leaders are displaying the very behaviours that are opposite to much of what we have been talking about as the BASICS of good leadership. Other research has noted the following pitfalls: relying on your promotion to give you power; acting on assumptions instead of clearly communicating your goals and asking for input and feedback; leading without being a good example; getting too comfortable in your position; and, ridding the workplace of fun.218 Th e process of educating, training and developing leaders is complex. Within the business sector, research indicates that most leadership training programs are not yielding the results that are needed.219 One-size-fi ts-all training programs are not providing the benefi ts one would hope for when developing younger and emerging leaders.220 What seems to be missing? In leadership expert Mike Myatt's view, training programs too oft en indoctrinate the learner in systems, processes, and techniques, and the experience can be rote, one-dimensional, and more of a monologue from the trainer than a dialogue with the participants.

***Ineffective leaders are not trusted; they operate with questionable integrity; they fail to consult others while leading; and, they ignore problems.***

Instead, we might do better to invest more in mentoring and coaching, and consider shift ing toward a developmental approach rather than a "cookie cutter" training program. It is also important to remember that not every good leader is a good teacher—sometimes it is useful to have the additional support from external professionals who excel in listening, facilitating, and encouraging open dialogue when training leaders. Th at can help ensure there is open, honest conversation that helps address questions, struggles, and areas of concern.

Considerations for Leadership Training If you and your organization are considering a leadership training or development program, ask yourself a few key questions: • How will we balance the need to develop skills and competencies with the need to develop character, a moral compass, and the inner core? • How will we create opportunities for dialogue, self-refl ection, and the fostering of selfawareness? • How will we encourage the development of emotional intelligence and soft skills? • How will we ensure we can provide activities that foster growth and development, along with opportunities to take in new information? • How will we access the latest fi ndings in neuroscience and other fi elds that are relevant to leadership development? It is also important to note that the employees who indicated the highest rates of satisfaction with their organization's leadership program were part of companies and organizations who invested signifi cant resources into their leadership programs, and had developed them over several years.

Selecting Leaders Selecting the right people to advance into leadership roles is critical for any sector, and especially in government roles. In the public sector, where job security oft en ensures tenure longevity, it is especially important to hire well and to promote well. Considerations for Hiring Here are a few questions to consider as you think about how your organization handles its hiring processes: • Are we looking for the right skills and attributes? • Are we taking enough time in our hiring processes? • Are we asking the right questions? • How well do we explore the mindset of the applicant? How can we assess their values, their moral compass? What do we know about their inner core? • Do we balance consistency with appropriate fl exibility when interviewing? Or do we force every applicant through the same process for consistency, even when that becomes counterproductive? (Consider the interviewer who says to an unsuccessful applicant: "I knew you knew the answer to this, but because you didn't say it aloud I couldn't give you the point." In a more fl exible process, the interviewer would be able to ask a question to draw out the knowledge that he knew the applicant possessed.) • How thoroughly do we explore their references? How else can we learn about them? It can be benefi cial to be able to recruit from within because you will have the benefi t of knowing the person and how well they fi t with the organization. Investing in succession planning and leadership development can be a solid strategy for helping to create the next generation of good leaders for your organization. Th is combines well with strategic external hires to ensure new ideas and approaches, to help prevent the organization from becoming entrenched, too inwardly focused, or out of touch.

## *Always do right. It will gratify some people and astonish the rest*

Final Thoughts Becoming a good leader is a journey that can last a lifetime. Good leaders never stop learning; their commitment to continuous learning and improvement drives them to continue. As you think about what you have learned in this book, think about how you can begin to implement the ideas and principles that are contained here. Th ink about the mindset you bring to work with you. What are your aspirations? What motivates you? What are your unspoken commitments that shape the kind of leader you have become? Our hope is that you will more seriously consider the deeper issues of leadership, and think more about what is at the very centre of who you are. Without that strong inner core, it will be diffi cult to lead well over time. We encourage you to build a strong moral compass, develop an ethical framework of principles that will guide you, and use those as a foundation upon which your competencies, aspirations and skills can be developed. Leaders who have these BASICS can be assured of greater success, and they have the satisfaction of knowing they will have a positive impact on those who follow them.

**Seriously consider the deeper issues of leadership, and what is at the centre of who you are.**

Commit to ongoing learning and growth. Becoming a good leader is a journey that can last a lifetime.